# How to plan exhibitions

By the same author

*Running a Successful Advertising Campaign*
*How to Plan Press Advertising*
*How to Plan Direct Mail*
*How to Plan Radio Advertising*
*The Perfect Conference*
*The Business Planner*
*Business Planning Made Simple*
*Successful Business Plans in a Week*
*Correct Letters*
*Instant Business Letters*
*Write That Letter!*
*Tricky Business Forms*
*Budgeting for Non-financial Managers*

# How to plan exhibitions

## Iain Maitland

CASSELL

**Cassell**
Wellington House, 125 Strand, London WC2R 0BB
PO Box 605, Herndon, VA 20172

First published 1997

**British Library Cataloguing-in-Publication Data**
A catalogue record for this book is available from the British Library.

ISBN 0-304-33431-6

Designed and typeset by Kenneth Burnley at Irby, Wirral, Cheshire.
Printed and bound in Great Britain by Redwood Books, Trowbridge, Wiltshire.

# Contents

# Acknowledgements

I WISH TO ACKNOWLEDGE the help of the following organizations which provided information of assistance in the compilation of this book. Special thanks are due to those which allowed me to reproduce their material in the text:

The Agricultural Show Exhibitors Association
The Association of Exhibition Organizers: in particular, Blanche Hunter
The Audit Bureau of Circulations Limited: in particular, Austen Hawkins
Batiste Publications Limited
The British Exhibition Contractors Association
Conference and Travel Publications Limited
Exhibition Audience Audits
Exhibition Surveys Limited
The Exhibition Industry Federation
The Incorporated Society of British Advertisers Limited
Inter Garden Promotions Limited
The National Exhibitors Association: in particular, Peter Cotterell
Target Response
TAS Exhibitions Limited
Themetree Limited: in particular, John Charlton
York Publishing Limited

To Tracey, Michael and Sophie

# Preface

How to plan exhibitions is aimed at you – the owner or manager of a potential, new or established small business who is planning to exhibit, probably for the first time. The text starts by introducing exhibitions to you. 'Types of exhibition' notes the characteristics, benefits and drawbacks of consumer, trade and private events. 'Who's who at exhibitions' discusses the main participants at an exhibition, representative bodies and other organizations which are involved with the industry.

Next, it details the background work that needs to be carried out by a would-be exhibitor. 'Thinking about yourself' tells you how to appraise your firm, assess products and services and check your goals. 'Recognizing your market' examines looking at your customers, judging rivals, studying your marketplace and conducting research. 'Setting a budget' shows you how to identify and analyse costs and estimate the expenditure which is likely to be required to finance your activities. Then, it moves on and takes you up to your first exhibition. 'Choosing exhibitions' covers shortlisting exhibitions, contacting organizers, making choices, booking space and drafting a timetable. 'Designing a stand' explains how to contemplate its appearance, select contents and compose a brief. 'Using specialists' spans commissioning a designer and employing a contractor.

The text ends by setting out many of the basic do's and don't's of exhibiting. 'Having a successful exhibition' guides you through maintaining your schedule, running the stand and evaluating results. 'The exhibitor's checklist' follows on with a comprehensive, step-by-step review of all the different stages which lead up to this winning conclusion.

Appendices are included at the back of the book. In-depth information about exhibitions, organizers, services, useful contacts and recommended reading form a highly valuable reference section. When linked with the chapter summaries, exhibition documents and glossary of key terms, this substantial back-up material completes this practical, hands-on guide to successful exhibiting.

*Iain Maitland*

# 1 Types of exhibition

SEVERAL TYPES OF EXHIBITION can be readily identified from the many thousands of events which are held in the United Kingdom and overseas each year. They may be grouped together loosely into three broad categories: consumer, trade and private shows. Initially, you should be aware of their basic characteristics as well as the possible benefits and drawbacks of exhibiting at them. Only then can you expect to press ahead to successfully plan, prepare for and attend those exhibitions which are most suited to your specific circumstances.

## Characteristics of exhibitions

Consumer shows are usually associated with products and services of widespread appeal as at the Holidays and Leisure Exhibition and the 'Which Computer?' Show. Anyone can attend – members of the public and tradespeople – so large numbers and diverse types of visitors are commonplace, the attendance of which is often audited at bigger, well-organized events. Admission may be free or, more likely, by ticket purchased in advance or on arrival. Such exhibitions can be held outdoors or indoors, from the grounds of a small hotel to the huge purpose-built exhibition centres in Birmingham, Glasgow and London.

Public shows may be considered to be local, with interest restricted to nearby residents; regional when people are drawn from up to 100 miles away; national with visitors coming from all areas of the country; or international when 20 per cent or more of exhibitors or visitors are from overseas. These events can be run by trade associations and/or professional exhibition organizers, such as Blenheim Events Limited and Nationwide Exhibitions Limited. Sometimes they are sponsored by another body as with the *Daily Mail*'s British Ski Show and Ideal Home Exhibition.

Trade exhibitions – often called business or technical events – are typically aimed at either everyone within a particular trade or industry or to a specific group (or groups) across a range of different industries. The Hospitality Exhibition and the Softworld in Personnel and Human Resources Exhibition are examples of such shows. Admission is often by invitation only so that a quality rather than a quantity attendance is assured, and strict registration and entry procedures are vigorously enforced so that this is achieved.

As with public exhibitions, these events can be held inside or outside, and may be referred to as local, regional, national or international. They are normally set up and administered by the appropriate trade body, perhaps in association with an experienced, professional exhibition organizer. Many shows have close links with a trade newspaper or magazine. As an example, the British International Toy and Hobby Fair is well publicized in the trade journal *Toy Trader*.

Sadly overlooked or at best ill-considered, private shows may be arranged for either public and/or trade visitors, depending upon the individual situation. All may be welcome, or admission could be strictly limited to a carefully chosen number of people such as trade buyers within the locality or region. Held outdoors or indoors from a tent, a mobile showroom or a hotel suite, these exhibitions are self-organized, perhaps in collaboration with other, complementary firms. Sometimes they are run close to related, national or international events in order to attract visitors from them.

## Benefits of exhibitions

There are many benefits to be derived from exhibiting at a show. Typically held on an annual or bi-annual basis, it is an exciting, looked-forward-to event: everyone is wondering what it will be like, who shall be there, what will be different and new, what may happen and so on. Just by being there, you can help to establish, change or maintain your reputation and status in the field. In many instances, you almost have to be present to 'keep up with the Joneses'. Your absence could be viewed – correctly or incorrectly – as a bad sign, possibly even of impending business failure.

Depending on the size of your stand, you may display a fuller range of goods than your sales team can take out on the road. Larger items – everything from an office photocopier to a mocked-up, one-bedroom starter home – may be shown too. Your products can be displayed as you want them to be seen, under controlled conditions. They may also be demonstrated, touched, tested, examined and operated by visitors. Supporting material from pattern swatches to promotional literature is readily available to hand. In theory, you can create the perfect sales environment.

Usually, a relaxed and informal show atmosphere exists at an event. For visitors, going to an exhibition is seen (perhaps naively by tradespeople) as an enjoyable, social occasion, or at least as a working holiday. They want to be there, are in a positive mood and are potentially interested in you and your goods and services. They have time to concentrate on you and what you have to show and say, without having other work to do, meetings to attend or telephone calls to take or make. In many respects, you have a captive and attentive audience.

An exhibition is a direct, face-to-face medium. You can meet past, present and prospective customers and talk, discuss products and services, ask and answer questions, negotiate, judge reactions and establish real, human relationships with them. Leads may be generated, contact lists built up, orders taken and sales made. Staff other than sales representatives can greet customers to exchange views and get to know each other better. If it is a busy show visited by the right people, you may meet more customers in one day than in weeks on the road.

Attending an exhibition also gives you the opportunity to research your market. You can discover what manufacturers, wholesalers, retailers, trade and statutory bodies are doing and planning, keep up-to-date with rivals and customers and identify changes, developments and trends in your area. In addition, you may find out what your customers think of you and – as important – your competitors and their products and services. In many ways, a show enables you to learn all about your trade in a short space of time.

Not surprisingly, each particular type of exhibition has its own individual benefits to offer to exhibitors. Consumer shows can be extremely busy, with a wide cross section of visitors, which may be what you want from an event. Trade exhibitions generally tend to have a smaller, tighter attendance containing a higher percentage of potential customers, assuming you have picked an appropriate show. Private events provide the greatest flexibility with regard to location, approach and price. Your customers are not distracted by other stands, nor can your rivals see what you are doing, as long as you carefully control and monitor entry to the exhibition.

## Drawbacks of exhibitions

Of course, various drawbacks can be attributed to exhibiting at an event and these need to be contemplated before going any further. A show may be set up for the wrong reasons. It could be organized simply because the owners of a hotel, hall or whatever want to promote their property as a would-be exhibition venue. It might be arranged to fill a venue during a seasonal lull. A trade association could launch a show to compete with a well-established and popular rival event. If an exhibition is not put on for the right reason – because there is a genuine demand for buyers and sellers to meet – then it is likely to fail, with insufficient numbers of exhibitors, visitors and so forth.

As in every industry, there are large numbers of 'cowboys' operating in the field. Some venue owners have totally unsuitable properties for the shows that they stage, perhaps being too small and with a complicated layout. Various organizers appear, take bookings and payments for events that never run, disappear and then re-appear at a later date in a different guise to begin the fraudulent process again. Numerous contractors – employed to bring the exhibition and exhibitors' stands to fruition – are qualified only in their desire to make quick money at everyone else's expense. These people steer clear of trade associations and their codes of conduct and recommended conditions of contract, and prey on naive exhibitors.

In many cases, exhibitions are just a wholly irrelevant medium for exhibiting firms. These exhibitors attend because it has not been tried before, a substantial discount has been offered to them and so on, rather than because it fits into their overall strategy and will help them to achieve their business objectives. Even if exhibiting is appropriate, it is hard to do well. You will find it difficult to choose the best exhibitions, book a quality site, create and design a winning stand. You are also very dependent upon others for your success – the venue owner, the organizer, contractors and even other exhibitors who must attend in the right numbers and mix to attract the necessary visitors.

The costs of exhibiting at any show are high. It is expensive to rent space, build a stand, arrange services, transport exhibits, book staff accommodation, promote your business before and after the event, and so on. Attending an exhibition also takes up the time and energies of senior, sales and other staff prior to, during and following the show, which might be better spent on alternative projects. Your routine may be disrupted for a significant period as well. As an example, sales representatives' usual cycles of visits to customers could be altered, with the possibility that orders might be seriously delayed or even lost.

Being on display hour after hour, day after day can be both a blessing and a curse for you. If your products begin to look tatty and staff start to lounge around then a negative impression will be conveyed and potential custom lost. Other stands can be an attraction too, with many exhibitors fighting to appeal to the same or very similar customers. Typically, visitors are also unwilling to place orders on site, preferring to see several stands and gather their thoughts together before making decisions. Unless you are ready to follow through with letters, phone calls and visits, hoped-for business can simply drift away once the excitement of the moment has passed.

Each specific type of show has its own particular drawbacks for exhibiting firms. Sometimes, both consumer and trade exhibitions become too large, having so many exhibitors that visitors cannot see all of the stands in one day. If there are large numbers of visitors, it is likely that only a very small percentage of them will be interested in you. Also, more popular stands and surrounding gangways can become busy, rapidly destroying the relaxed atmosphere. Private shows may be especially difficult to set up as you invariably have to take charge of everything yourself and must stand or fall by your own experience and abilities. It may also be hard to attract visitors, unless a rival event is being staged nearby.

## Summary

1. Exhibitions can be grouped together in three broad categories:
   - consumer shows
   - trade exhibitions
   - private events.

2. Many benefits may be derived from exhibiting at an event. In particular, an exhibition:
   - is an exciting, eagerly anticipated event
   - allows the perfect sales environment to be created
   - offers a relaxed and informal sales atmosphere
   - is a direct, 'face-to-face' medium
   - enables exhibitors to research their market.

3. Various drawbacks can be associated with exhibiting at an event. More specifically, an exhibition:
   - may be set up for the wrong reasons
   - could be operated by cowboys
   - might be unsuitable for some exhibitors
   - is often a costly marketing activity
   - is a time-consuming and tiring exercise.

4. It is important to consider the additional benefits and drawbacks concerning the following categories of exhibition:
   - consumer shows
   - trade exhibitions
   - private events.

# 2 Who's who at exhibitions

**M**ANY EXHIBITIONS are run along similar lines, with organizations and employees carrying out the same, basic roles at each of them. Various trade associations are active within the industry while numerous other bodies act in an advisory or regulatory capacity. You should know who is who at an exhibition and also be aware of these trade bodies and other organizations, and what they can do for would-be exhibitors such as yourself.

## At an exhibition

As a potential exhibitor, it is sensible to possess some background knowledge of:

- venue owners;
- exhibition organizers;
- designers;
- contractors;
- exhibitors;
- visitors.

### Venue owners

The individuals or company which owns the purpose-built centre, hall or showground will usually deal exclusively with the organizer of the show and will not come into contact with anyone exhibiting there at all. Clearly, they will have firm ideas about how the venue is and is not to be used though, and these will tend to be incorporated into the organizer's rules and regulations which exhibitors must adhere to in every way. See Chapter 6: 'Choosing exhibitions', page 47. Some venue owners belong to the trade body known as the British Exhibition Venues Association, page 9.

### Exhibition organizers

Many events are organized and run by the leading trade organization within a particular industry, such as the Building Societies Association and the

Camping and Outdoor Leisure Association. They are well established, trust-worthy and reliable and often have years of experience in the field. If you are a member of the association, you may obtain useful, hands-on advice and guid-ance as well as discounts on and first choice of the stands available at the venue.

Other events are administered by professional, exhibition management specialists. Larger, reputable ones are members of the trade body called the Association of Exhibition Organizers. See page 8. Smaller, less reputable ones tend to come and go, even conning money from would-be exhibitors with con-tracts for events which are never staged. All exhibition organizers need to be investigated carefully before money is handed over. Refer to Chapter 6: 'Choos-ing exhibitions', page 47.

### Designers

Professional designers – either freelance or employees of design groups – are commissioned by inexperienced but sensible exhibitors to design stands, advise on exhibits and display materials, and supervise their construction and installation at and removal from the exhibition floor. Care needs to be taken when choosing a designer and entering into a contractual obligation. See Chap-ter 8: 'Using specialists', page 82. Many first-rate designers belong to the Char-tered Society of Designers. Refer to Appendix D: 'Useful contacts', page 135.

### Contractors

Contractors – often nominated by the organizer or chosen individually by each exhibitor according to circumstances – are responsible for building stands under the supervision of the designers. They may also be responsible for other, associated services such as signwriting, painting and cleaning. Care has to be taken when selecting a contractor and signing a legally binding agreement. See Chapter 8: 'Using specialists', page 82. Some contractors are members of the trade body known as the British Exhibition Contractors Association, see page 9.

### Exhibitors

Not surprisingly, the majority of exhibitors will be in your industry, and many of them will be known to you; some may even be your direct rivals. Whether large or small, experienced or inexperienced, you will want to be sure that a good number and mix of exhibitors are present to draw in the right quan-tity *and* quality of visitors. You may also find that some exhibitors will be very open and helpful to you if approached, giving you useful information about their experiences. See Chapter 6: 'Choosing exhibitions', page 47. A small but growing number of exhibitors belong to the trade bodies called the Agricultural Show Exhibitors Association and National Exhibitors Association, see pages 8 and 10 respectively.

### Visitors

The people coming to the show will hopefully include a significant proportion of your existing and potential customers; there is little point in exhibiting if they will not be there. Refer to Chapter 6: 'Choosing exhibitions', page 47. The media will also be present, looking to report on the event, new products and services and any happenings of interest to their readers and listeners. You may want to tell them about yourself and your news. See Chapter 9: 'Having a successful exhibition', page 91.

## Representative bodies

There are numerous trade bodies which represent those organizations and people that are involved with exhibitions. You should be familiar with the following and the ways in which they can help you to become a successful exhibitor. Refer to Appendix D: 'Useful contacts', page 135, for addresses and telephone numbers.

- Agricultural Show Exhibitors Association
- Association of Exhibition Organizers
- British Exhibition Contractors Association
- British Exhibition Venues Association
- Exhibition Industry Federation
- National Exhibitors Association

### Agricultural Show Exhibitors Association

ASEA exists to serve the interests of its members at agricultural events, whether they are sole traders or multinational companies exhibiting in a shed or at a large pavilion. It is committed to maintaining the agricultural nature and content of shows as it believes that this type of event provides the best trade opportunity or public relations advantage for exhibitors. ASEA is constantly in contact with exhibition organizers, is represented on the committees of most major shows at county and national level, has representatives attending these events to aid members, and can offer advice and guidance based on a wide pool of knowledge and experience of agricultural shows.

### Association of Exhibition Organisers

AEO has four key objectives. It seeks to protect the interests of exhibition organizers in the United Kingdom by influencing venue owners on prices and developments and through liaising with the Government and European Union bodies on show issues. Second, it wants to increase awareness of exhibitions, promoting their value through research, publicity and training. The AEO also wishes to raise exhibition management standards in the United Kingdom by ensuring that its members adhere to its code of practice. Finally, it is currently seeking to secure another major London show venue by negotiating with and lobbying developers and local and national government.

The Association deals with enquiries about exhibitions, holds seminars and conducts training in show matters, all of which can be of considerable benefit to the would-be exhibitor. Its members also have to follow its code of practice and in most instances have to audit the attendance figures of the exhibitions to provide evidence of their professionalism and honesty. Clearly, these are reassuring signs for any firm thinking of exhibiting at an AEO member's event. Refer to Chapter 6: 'Choosing exhibitions', page 47.

### British Exhibition Contractors Association

BECA acts on behalf of contractors and suppliers who build and equip exhibition stands in the United Kingdom and overseas. Its main role is to protect its members' interests and to upkeep good standards of business practice, workmanship and service in the industry. As with most representative bodies, it will provide a list of its members on request, divided into operating areas such as signwriting, standfitting and so on. Also of interest to potential exhibitors, BECA members have to follow a code of practice and should issue contracts which match the Association's recommended conditions of contract. See Chapter 8: 'Using specialists', page 82 for more details.

### British Exhibition Venues Association

BEVA is a trade body that represents venue owners and tries to protect and enhance their image whilst furthering their interests within the exhibition industry. The Association offers free information and advice on its members and their facilities and services to those requiring suitable venues for exhibitions, and to would-be exhibitors as well. Refer to Chapter 6: 'Choosing exhibitions', page 47.

### Exhibition Industry Federation

EIF was created by venue owners, show organizers and contractors to improve communication within and increase business for the exhibition industry in the United Kingdom. Membership is restricted to trade bodies rather than companies or individuals. Of particular interest to the potential exhibitor, the Federation commissions research and publishes an annual report on exhibition statistics, covering volume, expenditure and effectiveness. In co-operation with the Department of Trade and Industry, it publishes an annual calendar of major United Kingdom trade fairs. Also, it organizes and promotes seminars and conferences on exhibition practice.

### National Exhibitors Association

NEA is run by exhibitors *for* exhibitors and has one overriding aim which is to increase the profitability of its members' exhibitions. It fights and campaigns for exhibitors on all fronts. For its members, it offers a helpline for impartial advice and guidance plus a low-cost, in-house consultancy service. Members are also entitled to substantial discounts on training courses dealing with subjects such as marketing strategies and stand design. Copies of a monthly newsletter *Exhibition File* are supplied free of charge.

## Other organizations

Other organizations are concerned with the exhibition industry. Addresses and telephone numbers are detailed in Appendix D: 'Useful contacts', page 135. Some of the largest are:

- Audit Bureau of Circulations Limited
- Exhibition Audience Audits
- Exhibition Surveys Limited
- Incorporated Society of British Advertisers Limited

### Audit Bureau of Circulations Limited

ABC is an independent, non-profit making company whose members include publishers, advertisers and advertising agencies. Its main role is to audit and certify the circulations of publications, such as newspapers and magazines. However, it also has an Exhibition Data Division which administers the auditing of exhibition attendance data in terms of quantity and quality. The auditing system produces what is known as a 'Certificate of Attendance' (COA) for the exhibition.

To achieve an ABC audit, members have to retain auditable records proving the attendance and demographic make-up of exhibition visitors. Audits are conducted to ABC rules and procedures by ABC's staff auditors or by chartered/certified audit firms, approved by ABC. The stringency of the audit is based on a full count of attendance and associated demographic data, and various checks being carried out to establish their accuracy such as reconciling registration cards with registered attendance and contacting a sample of claimed visitors to confirm they attended the event.

The results of each ABC exhibition audit are published as a 'Certificate of Attendance' (COA) which provides verification of the attendance at that exhibition and visitors' demographic details – in particular, their geographical locations, job titles and areas of company activity. The certificate also identifies the organizer, the sponsor (if appropriate), the date and venue of the show, the number of stands and space occupied, the date and venue of the next event, association membership (if applicable), target audience and products and services exhibited. An example of a Certificate of Attendance is shown on pages 12 to 15. Potential exhibitors ought to be wary of exhibiting at events which do not supply them with independently audited and verified figures, see Chapter 6: 'Choosing Exhibitions, page 47.

### Exhibition Audience Audits

EAA is an independent research consultancy specializing in the control of market research on behalf of exhibition organizers and exhibitors. In particular, it authenticates the total number of visitors to shows and produces audited attendance figures to standards approved by the Exhibition Industry Federation. Visitor research undertaken covers such areas as a detailed audience profile, audience interests, the overlap with competing shows and trends in the industry served by the exhibition. Research is also undertaken in exhibition development and management and the value of any special features and services.

### Exhibition Surveys Limited

This company specializes in industrial market research and aims to provide businesses with low-risk decision-making and marketing solutions. It is totally independent and has no connection with exhibition organizers, trade associations, publishers or exhibitors other than on a consultant/client basis. Working for small firms or multinational companies, it evaluates events for both organizers and exhibitors and supplies pre- and post-show information and advice on exhibition potential, audience quality, stand performance and so forth, customized to the individual client's requirements. See Chapter 6: 'Choosing exhibitions', page 47, and Chapter 9: 'Having a successful exhibition', page 91.

### Incorporated Society of British Advertisers Limited

ISBA represents national and international advertisers and seeks to promote quality advertising in all its many forms and at all times. It tries to help the exhibition industry to maintain and better its standards for the benefit of everyone involved. For example, it took the lead in improving the availability of reliable exhibition data by initiating the Certificate of Attendance administered by ABC. It also conducts an annual Exhibition Expenditure Survey based on a postal survey sent to exhibiting members and a selection of other exhibitors plus data collected from industry-wide sources. It attempts to assist would-be exhibitors to exhibit successfully by offering information and advice on request.

Exhibition News

## CERTIFICATE OF ATTENDANCE

## Exhibition News '96

| ORGANISER | ATTENDANCE | |
|---|---|---|
| Audit Bureau of Circulations | Registered Free | 6804 |
| Black Prince Yard | Registered Paid | 691 |
| 207-209 High Street | *Prior Year Registrations | 432 |
| Berkhamsted, Herts  HP4 1AD | Total Attendance | 7927 |

| | | % | |
|---|---|---|---|
| Tel No:    01442 870800 | *Prior Year Age Of Registration | % | |
| Fax No:   01442 877998 | Under 1 year | 92 | 396 |
| email:    abcpost@abc.org.uk | 1-2 years | 8 | 36 |
| Net:       http://www.abc.org.uk | 2-3 years | 0 | 0 |
| | Total Prior Year Attendance | 100 | 432 |

**SPONSOR**
ISBA

**STAND SPACE OCCUPIED: sq m 1843**
**NUMBER OF STANDS: 194**

**ORGANISERS ASSOCIATION MEMBERSHIP**
Association of Exhibition Organisers

**DATE OF EVENT:  6-8 March 1996**
**VENUE:   Royal Horticultural Halls**

**YEAR SHOW ESTABLISHED:  1976**
**FREQUENCY:  Annual**

**DATE OF NEXT EVENT:   4-6  March 1997**
**NEXT VENUE:  Royal Horticultural Halls**

**MAIN PRODUCT GROUPS/SERVICES  EXHIBITED**
Organisers, exhibitors, contractors and caterers involved in the exhibition industry.  Also trade media, training, marketing, research and allied services.

**TARGET AUDIENCE**
Managing Directors, Directors, Managers, Purchasers, Sales Executives, Advertising Agency and Media Personnel.

Page 1 of 4

**AUDITED ANALYSIS OF REGISTERED ATTENDANCE**

**Visitor Analysis by Geographical Area**

| DESCRIPTION | % | TOTAL |
|---|---|---|
| Northern | 15.0 | 1189 |
| Yorkshire & Humberside | 7.5 | 592 |
| North West | 22.5 | 1784 |
| East Midlands | 5.1 | 402 |
| Midlands | 6.7 | 534 |
| East Anglia | 11.9 | 943 |
| London | 1.3 | 104 |
| South East | 0.5 | 38 |
| South West | 1.2 | 97 |
| Wales | 3.5 | 277 |
| Scotland | 0.3 | 24 |
| Northern Ireland | 0.5 | 38 |
| TOTAL UK | 76.0 | 6022 |
| | | |
| OVERSEAS | | |
| | | |
| Europe - EU | 8.9 | 704 |
| Europe - Non EU | 1.1 | 89 |
| North America | 7.5 | 592 |
| Central & South America | 0.0 | 2 |
| Australasia & The Pacific | 2.3 | 184 |
| Asia | 1.2 | 94 |
| South East Asia & Pacific Rim | 1.0 | 84 |
| Africa | 1.6 | 127 |
| Middle East & North Africa | 0.4 | 29 |
| TOTAL OVERSEAS | 24.0 | 1905 |
| | | |
| TOTAL REGISTERED ATTENDANCE | 100.0 | 7927 |

**AUDITED ANALYSIS OF REGISTERED ATTENDANCE**

**Visitor Analysis by Job Function**

| DESCRIPTION | % | TOTAL |
|---|---|---|
| Chairman/Chief Executive | 4.8 | 383 |
| Managing Director | 14.4 | 1143 |
| Sales/Marketing Director | 8.6 | 682 |
| Director | 11.9 | 943 |
| Financial Director | 5.8 | 456 |
| Exhibition Manager | 10.2 | 809 |
| Other Manager | 19.0 | 1506 |
| Sales Executive | 7.2 | 572 |
| Consultant | 7.6 | 601 |
| Agency Personnel | 2.2 | 169 |
| Student | 1.1 | 87 |
| Other | 4.7 | 374 |
| Unspecified | 2.5 | 202 |
| | 100.0 | 7927 |

**Visitor Analysis by Company Activity**

| DESCRIPTION | % | TOTAL |
|---|---|---|
| Exhibition Organiser | 37.9 | 3004 |
| Stand Design | 37.0 | 2930 |
| Contractor | 22.5 | 1784 |
| Caterer | 4.1 | 327 |
| Sales/Marketing Agency | 6.0 | 479 |
| Consultant | 9.3 | 740 |
| Other | 4.3 | 342 |
| Unspecified | 1.3 | 104 |
| | | 9710 |

Note: Analysis allows for multiple responses by the attendee

## AUDITED ANALYSIS OF REGISTERED ATTENDANCE

### Visitor Analysis by Company Size

| NUMBER OF EMPLOYEES | % | TOTAL |
|---|---|---|
| Under 10 | 12.4 | 984 |
| 11 - 20 | 24.6 | 1948 |
| 21 - 50 | 31.1 | 2462 |
| 51 - 100 | 15.8 | 1248 |
| 101 - 250 | 2.9 | 231 |
| 251 - 500 | 2.8 | 222 |
| 501 - 1000 | 2.1 | 169 |
| 1001 + | 5.0 | 400 |
| Unspecified | 3.3 | 263 |
| | 100.0 | 7927 |

ABC Reference Number: 001

All data published in this Certificate of Attendance has been audited to the standards laid down by the ABC Exhibition Industry Working Party and is authorised for issue by the Exhibition Division of the Audit Bureau of Circulations Ltd (by Guarantee).

No figures may be published without the permission of the copyright holders.

Although every care is taken to ensure that the information published is correct the Audit Bureau of Circulations cannot accept responsibility for mistakes or omissions.

Published by ABC, Black Prince Yard,
207-209 High Street, Berkhamsted,
Herts, HP4 1AD
Phone (01442) 870800  Fax (01442) 877998
email: abcpost@abc.org.uk  Net: http://www.abc.org.uk

**Authorised for issue by the ABC**

**1st March 1996**

**ABC**
AUDIT BUREAU OF CIRCULATIONS
**EXHIBITIONS**

## 1. INTRODUCTION

1.1   The purpose of the ABC Exhibition audit is to give prospective exhibitors, advertisers, sponsors and other interested parties an independent and comparable guide of the past performance of an exhibition to enable them to gauge its likely future performance.

1.2   The Audit Bureau of Circulations (ABC) was founded in 1931 as a non profit making organisation by advertisers who wanted an independent standard for the validation of circulation and attendance data. ABC now provides, to the highest standards in the world, accurate, objective and comparable figures on over 3,000 member titles and exhibitions.

1.3   ABC is managed by a full-time staff governed by a general council of members representing advertisers, agencies, organisers and publishers. Working Parties and ABC staff representing each category of membership, continually monitor the rules and procedures appropriate to each category to ensure that they reflect the needs of members and the industry at large.

1.4   The audits are conducted to ABC rules and procedures by ABC's own staff who are responsible for certifying audit returns, visiting organisers and their registration bureaux to check the audit rules and procedures are fully adhered to.

1.5   ABC has been certifying trade exhibition attendance since 1976. In 1993 the two previous audit schemes were consolidated into the Certificate of Attendance (COA). The COA has quickly become the industry standard for the provision of quantitative and qualitative trade exhibition attendance data.

1.6   The Exhibition Organiser is responsible for producing the attendance data, maintaining proper records and completing the ABC Certificate of Attendance return and has a duty of care to the Bureau.

1.7   ABC must have full and free access to all relevant financial and other records connected with the audit of the exhibition, as far as may be necessary to conduct the audit in accordance with notes and instructions herein.

## 2. REGISTRATION

2.1   Registration for a Consumer Event Certificate of Attendance (hereafter referred to as the COA) must take place before the start of the exhibition and should, ideally, take place 6 months in advance of the exhibition.

2.2   Registration of the exhibition must be approved by the Bureau in writing.

2.3   The exhibitor pack detailing stand space costs should be submitted with the registration form or as soon as it is available.

2.4   The exhibition catalogue should be sent with the registration form or as soon as it is available.

2.5   The complimentary ticket (if applicable) should be approved by the Bureau. They must be submitted with the registration form as soon as it is available.

---

**ABC audit rules – consumer events**

2.6    A Stand Plan detailing the length and width of each stand should be submitted with the registration form or as soon as it is available.

2.7    Having registered an exhibition for a COA, the Organiser is committed to the audit and completion of the certificate unless the show is cancelled or the show attendance is affected by circumstances outside the organisers' control. Non completion will result in the exhibition registration being formally terminated by ABC.

However Organisers registering for their first audit may elect for a 'Trial Audit' which will not commit them to publishing their registration for the audit or the results.

**2.8    Once an exhibition is registered with ABC, the registration stands until the Organiser specifically resigns that registration (i.e. subsequent equivalent events are committed to completing COA's unless a resignation is properly effected). The resignation must for, Annual shows be tendered at least 6 calendar months before the first day of the next show and for bienniel shows 12 months in advance of the show.**

2.8.1  For all subsequent events the Organiser must submit a completed Permanent Information Form 6 months before the first day of the show. The event catalogue and stand plan detailing the length and width of the stands must be submitted with this Permanent Information Form or as soon as they are available.

2.9    An exhibition which has had its registration terminated, may not, even after reapplication for an exhibition audit use the ABC logo in pre-show publicity until a new certificate has been issued.

## 3.   CERTIFICATION

The Certificate will analyse the attendance by different entrance fee levels as follows:

| | |
|---|---|
| Full Price | Visitors who gain access to the show via payment of the advertised full price admission fees. |
| Concessions | Visitors who gain access to the show at a reduced rate to those advertised. |
| Bulk Sales | A sale of two or more tickets resulting in such tickets being given, free of charge, to the visitor. |
| Complimentary | Visitors who gain access to the show free of charge. |
| Exhibitor personnel | Exhibition staff who man the stands may, as an option,be reported on the certificate. Exhibitor personnel will be included in the total net attendance. |

## 4.    INSPECTION

4.1    An Exhibition Organiser must, on application by the Bureau, allow any authorised representative of the Bureau access within seven days to all or any records necessary to check the accuracy of a COA.

4.2    The Bureau reserves the right to visit a registered exhibition at any time to observe entry and recording procedures. The Organiser, at this time, must grant free access to the authorised representative of the Bureau to the exhibition and all relevant records.

## 5.   PUBLICITY/REPRODUCTION OF THE COA

5.1   ABC strongly recommends the earliest possible registration of the exhibition as this allows maximum use of promotional opportunities.

**5.2   ALL promotional material that makes reference to ABC must be approved by ABC, in writing, prior to release.**

5.3   Any figures quoted near the ABC logo, on any material, must be the latest figures certified by ABC and the dates of the show must be stated. The attendance total must also show the breakdown between free and paid attendees.

5.4   Any attendance figures or statements which are made in publicity material that include the ABC logo must be presented in such a way that it is clear which information has and which information has not been certified by ABC.

5 5   Following successful completion of the COA audit, ABC will produce the original COA from the audited data provided. Copies may be reproduced by the Organiser from the aforementioned original or ABC can provide copies at cost. All copies must be reproduced in the format of the original certificate produced by ABC.

## 6.   TIME LIMIT FOR SUBMISSION OF THE COA

6.1   The completed COA return must be received by the Bureau within 45 days of the last day of the exhibition. Late submissions will be subject to a surcharge of £100.

6.2   The surcharge must be paid and the COA must be submitted within 14 days of the date of issue of the late submission invoice, otherwise the exhibition registration will be formally terminated by ABC. Any such termination will be entered in the ABC newsletter, Update.

## 7.   QUALIFIED PAID ATTENDANCE

Qualified Paid Attendance will be the number of visitors who gain access to the show by paying an admission charge only. The Paid attendance will be evaluated by reconciling the cash collected against the counted attendance. To facilitate this reconciliation the following financial/attendance records, audit rules and procedures must be adhered to.

Paid attendance is split into two main categories, visitors who purchase their entrance ticket at the exhibition (on-site) and visitors who purchase their ticket before the start of the exhibition (advance). To allow ABC to audit the counted paid attendance, and the cash collected for on-site and advance/attendance ticket sales, the following audit rules and procedures will apply:

7.1   ON-SITE TICKET SALES

The following audit rules apply to tickets purchased at the show.

7.1.1   **Ticket Books/Fan Tickets**

Ticket books or fan tickets **must** be used to count the paid attendance.

7.1.2   All claimed on-site paid attendees **must** purchase an entrance ticket from the ticket box office at the show.

7.1.3   The attendee will surrender the ticket to gain entrance to the show. The Organiser will either collect the whole ticket from the visitor or tear the ticket, retaining one portion and returning the other portion to the visitor.

7.1.4 ABC does **NOT** require on-site tickets to be retained by the Organiser, however if they are, they must be stored separately from advance tickets.

7.1.5 Each ticket book must have its own unique sequential number range printed on the tickets.

7.1.6 Separate identifiable ticket books with unique number ranges must be used for each payment rate available to gain access to the exhibition (i.e. full rate (adult), 75% of full rate (student), 50% of full rate (child/OAP) etc.).

7.1.7 Each cashier should be given a specific number of ticket books. The unique ticket number range should be recorded and signed for by the cashier and the Organiser's accountant/supervisor. The cashiers should only sell the batch of tickets they signed for.

7.1.8 Unsold tickets must be returned to and retained by the Organiser. The number of returned tickets and their unique number range must be recorded and signed for by the cashier and the Organiser's accountant/supervisor.

7.1.9 The unique ticket numbers of the first ticket and the last ticket sold in the period **must** be recorded on the relevant cashier sheet. See audit rule 7.5 and sample cashier sheet A1.

7.1.10 **"The Period"** referred to in these rules relates to the life span of a cashiers sheet. A cashiers sheet is completed and a new one started each time the organiser's supervisor or accountant collects cash from the cashier.

7.1.11 The counted paid attendance, for ABC purposes, can be calculated using ticket books only. However, as an option, Organiser may wish to use any or all of the listed below, in conjunction with ticket books, to count the paid attendance.

7.2 Ticketing Machines

7.2.1 The machines used to dispense and count the on-site entrance tickets issued to visitors **should** be used in conjunction with ticket books to count the paid attendance.

7.2.2 All on-site entrance tickets will be sold through the ticket box office and should be despatched via a ticketing machine.

7.2.3 The counters on the ticketing machine will be read at the start and the finish of the period and recorded together with the unique ticket numbers on the relevant cashiers sheet.

7.3. Till Rolls

7.3.1 As an option Organisers **may** elect to use Till rolls in conjunction with ticket books to count the paid attendance.

7.3.2 If so, all sales of entrance tickets must be cashed via a till which can record the transactions on a till roll.

7.3.3 The number of ticket sales on the till must be recorded on the cashier sheet and all the till rolls attached to the relevant cashiers sheets.

7.4 Turnstile

7.4.1 As an option Organisers **may** elect to use turnstiles in conjunction with ticket books to count the paid attendance.

7.4.2 If so, all visitors must pass through a turnstile when entering the exhibition. The counters must be read at least at the start and finish of each day.

7.4.3 The counter reading must be recorded and signed as correct by the reader.

7.5    **Cash sheets**

7.5.1  For each cashier, a cash sheet recording and reconciling the cash collected against the counted attendance must be maintained. A cash sheet must be completed and a new one started each time cash is collected by the organisers from the cashier and passed for banking.

7.5.2  The cash sheet must, as a minimum, make provision for the capture of the data listed below. Please see sample enclosed cashier sheet reference Al. If you wish to use this form please contact the Bureau for copies or photocopy the attached.

- Exhibition title and date
- Cashier's name and window position
- Float
- Opening number, closing number and total number of tickets issued for each payment rate available to gain access to the show. If all the tickets are sold, a 2nd batch of tickets will be issued to the cashier. The opening and closing numbers and total number of tickets issued must be recorded separately on the cash sheet. Please see column headings "lst batch ticket book" and "2nd batch ticket book" as an example on attached cash sheets reference A1.
- Opening number, closing number and total number of tickets dispensed per the ticket machine (if applicable).
- Till Rolls (if applicable).
- Value of tickets sold
- Cash collected, cheques collected, voucher value, credit card total.
- Cashier's signature and supervisor's signature.
- Cash analysis, voucher analysis.

7.5.3  Obviously the frequency of completion of the cash sheets will be dependent upon the visitor flow at the show. Some shows may require several cash sheets to be completed per cashier per day, whereas other shows will only require 1 or 2. However, as a minimum, each cashier must complete one cash sheet per day.

7.5.4  Where multiple cash sheets are completed each day, a daily cash sheet summary form should be completed. This summary sheet must, as a minimum, include the data listed below. Please see sample enclosed cash sheet summary form reference A2. If you wish to use this form, please contact the Bureau for copies or photocopy the attached.

- Exhibition title and date
- Cashier's name and window position
- Type of ticket, payment rate, number of tickets sold.
- Each cash sheet (A1) must be given a unique reference number. This number or range of numbers (if multiple cash sheets are completed each day) will be recorded on the Daily Cash summary form (A2).

7.6    BANKING SHEETS

7.6.1  A banking sheet must be completed each time ticket money is banked. The sheet must, as a minimum, include the data listed below. Please see sample enclosed banking sheet form reference B 1. If you wish to use the form please contact the Bureau or photocopy the attached.

- Exhibition title and date
- Cashier's name and window position
- Cash collected per cashier and total amount banked

7.6.2    ABC strongly recommends that ticket sales are banked separately from catalogue sales and other miscellaneous income. However if this is not the case then the above banking sheet must include a breakdown of the cash banked, for example:

| | |
|---|---|
| Ticket sales | £ |
| Catalogue sales | £ |
| Poster sales | £ |
| Miscellaneous | £ |

7.6.3    Where multiple banking sheets are completed each day, a daily banking sheet summary form should be completed. This summary sheet should, as a minimum, include the data listed below. Please see sample enclosed banking sheet summary form reference B2. If you require copies of this form please contact the Bureau or photocopy the attached form.

- Exhibition name and date
- Cashiers' names and window positions
- Banking sheet Reference number(s)
- Value of tickets sold per cashier, revenue collected per cashier
- Total value of tickets sold, total revenue
- Total banked, time of banking, revenue analysis.

7.7    **VOUCHERS**

7.7.1    To facilitate the audit of visitors who gain entrance to the show at a reduced rate via submission of a voucher, the following will apply.

7.7.2    The visitor must surrender the voucher to the cashier when purchasing the entrance ticket.

7.7.3    If multiple types of vouchers are available to gain reduced rate entrance, they must be separated and counted on a daily basis. The number of vouchers collected will be recorded and analysed on the cash sheet. The vouchers must be kept in their counted bundles with a note detailing the number of vouchers held in the bundle. ABC will sample check the voucher count.

7.7.4    With the exception of a family voucher, a single voucher may only allow one reduced payment entry. One voucher CANNOT allow multiple visitors reduced rate entrance.

A family voucher may only allow a set discount for a set number of Adult and Child visitors, i.e. Two Adults and Two Children may gain entrance at X reduced rate fee with submission of the voucher. The number of adult and child visitors who gain reduced rate entrance on a family voucher will be set by the Organiser.

The number of reduced rate visitors who gain entrance via submission of a family voucher ticket will exactly match the number of reduced rate visitors per the family vouchers collected from the visitors on entrance to the show. ABC will sample count these vouchers.

7.7.5    A single voucher may only give one rate of discount. It CANNOT give one discount for an adult visitor and a different rate for a child visitor.

7.7.6    Daily voucher sheets should also be completed. The sheet should, as a minimum, include the data listed below. Please see sample enclosed daily vouchers sheet reference C1. If you require copies of this form please contact the Bureau or photocopy attached.

- Exhibition name and date

- Source of voucher (i.e. Daily Mail, News magazine)
- Value of each type of voucher
- Total number of each type of voucher

7.8    ADVANCE TICKET SALES

The following audit rules apply to entrance tickets purchased in advance of the show.

**Ticket Books**

7.8.1    Ticket books **must** be used to count the advance paid attendance.

7.8.2    All claimed advance paid attendees **must** purchase an entrance ticket from an official outlet, e.g. Organiser box office, ticket agency, British Rail, etc.

7.8.3    The attendee must surrender the ticket to gain entrance to the show. The Organiser must collect and retain the whole or the stubb of the ticket from the visitor. If the Organiser collects the stubb of the ticket only that section of the ticket may be counted towards the attendance. If the wrong section of the ticket is collected it will be excluded from the counted attendance.

7.8.4    Each sales outlet must have a separately identifiable ticket. If variable entrance rates are available from a single ticket outlet, the entrance rate must be printed on each ticket.

7.8.5    Advance tickets must be retained and stored separately from on-site tickets.

7.8.6    The various ticket types and payment rates must be separated and counted on a daily basis. The number of advance tickets collected will be recorded and analysed on the advance ticket sales sheet.

7.8.7    The advance tickets must be kept in their counted daily bundles with a note detailing the number of tickets held in the bundle. ABC will sample check the ticket counts.

7.9    Advance Ticket Sales Sheet

An advance ticket sales sheet detailing the number of tickets sold by each ticket outlet must be maintained. The advance ticket sales sheet must, as a minimum, include the data listed below. Please see attached sample enclosed advance ticket sales sheet reference DI. If you require copies of this form please contact the Bureau or photocopy attached.

- Exhibition name and date
- Ticket sales outlets
- Ticket type and payment rate
- Total number of tickets collected
- Total value of tickets collected

7.10    Bulk Ticket Sales

A sale of two or more tickets resulting in such tickets being given, free of charge, to the visitor.

Examples include sales to exhibitor, airlines, hotels, business, etc.

8.    **QUALIFIED FREE ATTENDANCE**

Qualified free attendance will be the number of visitors who gain access to the show free of charge and adhere to the audit rules below:

**8.1    Ticket Books/Registration Cards**

8.1.1    Ticket books/registration cards must be used to count the free attendance.

8.1.2    The attendee must surrender a ticket to gain access to the show. The Organiser must collect and retain the whole ticket from the visitor. The complimentary tickets must be stored separately from on-site and advance tickets.

8.1.3    The collected complimentary tickets must, as a minimum, be counted on a daily basis. The counts must be recorded on the advance ticket sales sheet. The tickets must be stored in their counted daily bundles with a note detailing the number of tickets in the bundle. ABC will sample check the ticket counts.

8.1.4    The Organiser must also comply with ONE of the following two criteria listed below:

- The complimentary entry ticket must include the name of the show and make provision for the capture of the visitor's name, address, postcode and telephone number.

- Only complimentary entry tickets surrendered by the visitor to gain access to the show which have captured the name and address will be included on the certificate.

**OR**

- Each ticket book must have its own unique sequential number range printed on the tickets.

- The Organiser maintains a record of who the complimentary tickets were sent to. The record will include the name, company name, address, telephone number, number of tickets, and the tickets unique reference number or range of numbers. ABC will, on a sample basis, cross reference the unique number held on those complimentary tickets (collected from free visitors on entrance to the show) to unique reference numbers recorded by the Organiser. ABC will also contact a random sample of the companies held on the list to seek their verification of receipt of the complimentary tickets.

**8.2    Exhibitor Personnel**

The Exhibition Organiser may, as an option, report the number of attending exhibitor personnel, providing auditable records are held to support inclusion of the data (i.e. exhibitor registration cards). Exhibitor personnel will be included in the total net attendance.

**9.    TOTAL ATTENDANCE & REVENUE SUMMARY SHEETS**

9.1    To allow ABC to reconcile the total attendance against the total cash/vouchers collected, the Organiser must collate the various sheets maintained for the duration of the show into a accurate summary of the visitor attendance and the revenue generated from ticket sales.

9.2    The attendance summary must, as a minimum, include the data listed below. Please see enclosed sample attendance summary sheet reference E1. If you require copies of this sheet please contact the Bureau or photocopy attached.

- Exhibition name and date
- Number of visitors per day analysed by type of attendance ticket

9.3     The ticket revenue summary must, as a minimum, include the data listed below. Please see enclosed revenue summary sheet reference F1. If you require copies of this form please contact the Bureau for copies or photocopy attached.

- Exhibition name and date
- Type of ticket and payment rate
- Number of tickets sold
- Revenue collected
- Revenue invoiced

## 10.    RECORDS TO BE HELD

10.1    All records listed and any further records financial or otherwise needed to ensure the accuracy of the ABC Certificate must be held until the ABC certificate for the subsequent show has been audited by ABC. All records must be available for audit or inspection at any time and within 7 days of request by ABC or its appointed representatives.

10.2    All financial records relating to ticket sales and stand sales including invoices, credit notes, paying in books and bank statements must be made available to ABC for inspection at any time within 7 days of ABC's request. If there is any doubt as to what should be held, the Organiser should contact ABC. The aim of the rule is to ensure that the audit can be conducted from the retained records.

10.3    All vouchers, advance and complimentary tickets must be separated by ticket design and stored with a record of the number of tickets held in each batch and on what day the tickets were collected.

10.4    All records maintained to count and record the counted paid attendance and cash collected, i.e. cash sheets, banking sheets, etc.

## 11.    NUMBER OF STANDS AND STANDS SPACE OCCUPIED

11.1    The COA will certify the Total Stand Space Occupied.

11.2    Stand Space Occupied will include all exhibition stands available to all attendees, whether paid, free or obtained via a contra deal. It shall NOT include rest areas, restaurants, conference rooms, exhibitor lounges etc.

11.3    The COA will certify the Total Number of Stands. The Organiser must hold auditable contractual evidence for each stand shown on the COA.

11.4    The Stand Plan submitted with the registration form (see Audit Rule 2.5) should be coded to indicate which stands have been sublet and the number of sublessees.

11.5    Any stands that have been divided by sub-letting by the original contracted exhibitor may only be included as additional stands on the COA under the following circumstances:

11.6    The catalogue reflects entries for those on the shared stand area or the original contracted exhibitor provides written evidence of the division of the stand.

11.7    The Bureau is satisfied that the stand space clearly allows the individual exhibitors to be identified and located within the divided area. In any cases of doubt the Bureau will decide.

11.8    The Organiser must submit, with the return, an exhibitor list detailing the exhibitor's company name, stand number, stand dimension and stand space occupied.

11.9    **Feature Area Stand Space** may, as an option, be included on the certificate as a separate figure, i.e. feature areas stand space will not be included in the mandatory exhibitor stand space figure.

## 12.    COMPLAINTS PROCEDURES

12.1.    Any complaint made against an Organiser shall be in writing addressed to the ABC Chief Executive.

12.2.    The Chief Executive shall, if he considers that a prima facie case for complaint exists, refer the complaint to the Exhibition Organiser complained of who shall have the right to make a written statement in answer within fourteen days.

12.3.    If the ABC Chief Executive finds a complaint against an Organiser well founded, he may withdraw any ABC COA already issued and/or that Exhibition Organiser may be censured, suspended temporarily and/or subject to the fulfilment of such conditions as the Bureau may impose or may terminate the exhibition registration. Such decisions of the Chief Executive shall be notified to all ABC members and such other parties as the ABC sees fit in the interest of protecting the reputation of the ABC.

12.4.    If, in the opinion of the Chief Executive, a complaint is well founded, the Bureau will pay the costs of any re-audit incurred in connection with the complaint. The Bureau will recover such costs from the offending Organiser unless otherwise agreed by the Chief Executive. If in the opinion of the Chief Executive a complaint is not well founded, the complainant will pay the costs of re-audit plus 20% thereof to cover the Bureau's expenses.

## Summary

1. Numerous interested organizations and individuals are likely to be present at an exhibition, including:
   - venue owners
   - exhibition organizers
   - designers
   - contractors
   - exhibitors
   - visitors.

2. There are various trade bodies in existence, which represent different interests within the industry. In particular:
   - Agricultural Show Exhibitors Association
   - Association of Exhibition Organizers
   - British Exhibition Contractors Association
   - British Exhibition Venues Association
   - Exhibition Industry Federation
   - National Exhibitors Association.

3. An assortment of other organizations are involved in some way with the exhibition industry, incorporating:
   - Audit Bureau of Circulations Limited
   - Exhibition Audience Audits
   - Exhibition Surveys Limited
   - Incorporated Society of British Advertisers Limited.

# 3 Thinking about yourself

**W**HETHER YOU ARE THINKING of exhibiting at a consumer, trade or private show, you must begin your preparations by contemplating your firm, products, services and goals. When linked with an awareness of your market and an understanding of the costs of exhibiting, such a self-assessment will provide you with the basic information required to decide which exhibitions to choose and how to exhibit at them. Alternatively, this initial groundwork may indicate that exhibitions are unsuitable in your specific circumstances.

## Appraising your firm

Every would-be exhibitor should have a full and detailed knowledge of his or her business, being wholly familiar with its organization and workings from top to bottom. If you do do not already possess a hands-on appreciation of your concern, discover all there is to know about the type of business it is, the way it is structured, what its policies are, how it operates, the roles and responsibilities of different departments and employees, and so on. Understand your firm inside out before proceeding any further.

Recognizing the particular strengths and weaknesses of your concern is a pre-requisite for any successful marketing campaign. Consider and note down your firm's qualities. Typically, these might include: an ideal location to supply goods to customers, always being fully stocked, and a prompt and friendly after-sales service. Think about and list its shortcomings too. These could incorporate an overdependence on its owner managers, limited financial resources and a lack of experience in advertising and promotional methods.

Combining your assessment of the business with an awareness of exhibitions – see Chapter 1: 'Types of exhibition', page 1 – should allow you to draw one or two preliminary conclusions about your choice of exhibitions and possible tactics. As examples, relying on key staff to do everything, severe financial restraints and inexperience may suggest that highly professional and costly consumer and trade events are inappropriate in this instance. A modest private show at which the firm's site, stock levels and after-sales service are promoted could be more fitting. Completing the form, 'Appraising your firm: an action checklist' on page 28 at this point will be beneficial.

## THE FIRM

| Characteristics | Its qualities | Its shortcomings |
| --- | --- | --- |
| 1. Type | | |
| 2. Structure | | |
| 3. Policies | | |
| 4. Operations | | |
| 5. Departments | | |
| 6. Employees | | |
| 7. Other features | | |

## EXHIBITIONS

Characteristics:

Benefits:

Drawbacks:

**Appraising your firm: an action checklist**

## PRODUCTS AND SERVICES

| | **Positive features** | **Negative features** |
|---|---|---|
| 1. Types | | |
| 2. Varieties | | |
| 3. Uses | | |
| 4. Packaging | | |
| 5. Prices | | |
| 6. Durability | | |
| 7. Guarantees | | |
| 8. Other features | | |

## EXHIBITIONS

Characteristics:

Advantages:

Disadvantages:

**Assessing your products and services: an action checklist**

**THE BUSINESS**

| Short-term goals | Medium-term goals | Long-term goals |
| --- | --- | --- |
| 1. | 1. | 1. |
| 2. | 2. | 2. |
| 3. | 3. | 3. |
| 4. | 4. | 4. |
| 5. | 5. | 5. |
| 6. | 6. | 6. |
| 7. | 7. | 7. |
| 8. | 8. | 8. |
| 9. | 9. | 9. |

**EXHIBITIONS**

Characteristics:

Pros:

Cons:

**Checking your goals: an action checklist**

## Assessing your products and services

Next, you must study your existing and planned range of goods and services. Find out all you can about the different types and varieties, what they are used for, how they are packaged and priced, how well established they are, what guarantees are given with them and so forth. The products or services you are selling are of prime significance as they will be displayed or featured on your exhibition stand and can make or break its success; refer to Chapter 7: 'Designing a stand', page 77.

Taking each product or service in turn, set down its positive features. Hopefully, it meets customers' requirements, does what it is supposed to do, is competitively priced and is available on request. Be ready to promote these qualities at the exhibition. Sketch out its negative aspects too, seeking to remedy them so far as possible. However well displayed and competently staffed your stand may be, you will not be able to sell unwanted or sub-standard goods or services.

Looking at your products and services will enable you to think further about the events that you may attend and the techniques which could be employed there. Seasonal goods might suggest summer rather than winter shows, or vice versa. Large and heavy items could restrict you to outdoor rather than indoor events or might even rule out exhibitions altogether if they are difficult to move and are better viewed on site. Knowing what you want to display may also indicate the size of stand needed, its layout and so on. See Chapter 6: 'Choosing exhibitions', page 47. Refer to 'Assessing your products and services: an action checklist' on page 29 for more assistance.

## Checking your goals

Consider next your firm's future, making certain that you are totally aware of what you wish to achieve on a short-, medium- and long-term basis. You should contemplate attending exhibitions only if they fit in with your overall plans and help you to move significantly towards your business goals. Knowing where you want to go also enables you to select appropriate exhibitions and to take the right approach to them, by providing parameters to work within and targets to aim for.

Write out your various key objectives. For the immediate future, you may wish to launch a new product onto an existing market, generating total sales of £100,000 within the first year, from a minimum of 100 retail accounts. In the mid-term, your goals could incorporate selling direct to end users through mail order catalogues, producing an annual turnover of £200,000. For the distant future, you could want to relaunch your modified product into an overseas marketplace, obtaining £500,000 sales per annum, and so forth.

Once more, a thorough examination of your aims gives you the opportunity to formulate some provisional ideas about would-be shows and tactics, and whether exhibitions are fitting in your situation. Clearly, an exhibition is an effective way of launching an innovative product, and targeting retail accounts points to the maximization of trade events. Subsequently expanding sales to end users suggests the use of consumer shows, with international events being attended to promote goods to foreign buyers. Take a look at 'Checking your goals: an action checklist' on page 30 at this stage. You may find it useful.

## Summary

1. Potential exhibitors should begin their preparations by considering their firm, products, services and goals. This initial groundwork – when combined with follow-up activities – will enable them to:
   - decide whether or not exhibitions are a suitable medium in the circumstances
   - choose appropriate exhibitions, if relevant
   - calculate how to exhibit at exhibitions.

2. A would-be exhibitor's assessment of their own firm should focus on:
   - all aspects of the business, from top to bottom
   - its particular strengths and weaknesses
   - the relationship between the firm's strengths and weaknesses and exhibitions' benefits and drawbacks.

3. An appraisal of goods and services should be concerned with:
   - their main features
   - the positive and negative aspects of these different features
   - how the particular products and services affect the choice of and approach to exhibitions, and vice versa.

4. Prospective exhibitors need to check their goals, which involves:
   - listing exactly what they want to achieve
   - classifying goals into the short, medium and long terms
   - comparing and contrasting goals with the benefits and drawbacks of exhibiting, to see how suited they are.

# 4 Recognizing your market

**M**OVING AHEAD WITH YOUR GROUNDWORK, you must familiarize yourself with the market in which you operate. Find out as much as possible about your current and prospective customers, rivals and the marketplace itself. Again, this preparatory work, carried out by all sensible exhibitors, should enable you to decide whether exhibitions really are right for your firm. If they seem to be, it may also further substantiate and add to your thoughts about the types of show to attend and how to approach them.

## Looking at your customers

Try to build up a clear image of your customers. If you trade with other businesses, check out who they are, where they are based and what they do. Should you deal with members of the public, discover who they are and whether they are male or female, young or old, married or unmarried, with or without children as well as where they live, what they do for a living, what they earn, what interests they have and so forth. Do not forget that although you might trade with fellow concerns, they may sell your goods to the general public, in which case you should possess a broad picture of both firms and end users – the buyers *and* the influencers.

In addition, learn all you can about what your customers purchase, as well as why, where, when and how often. Get to know their opinions of your business, products and services, and see if their perceptions of your positive and negative features match your own assessments. Find out what they think of your competitors and their goods and services. Also ascertain whether they attend exhibitions. If they do, check on which ones, why, when and how often. Whatever your advertising or promotional activities, you can never know too much about the concerns and/or people you are attempting to sell to.

Having an understanding of your customers' characteristics and habits – pieced together from your contacts with them, existing records and extra communications – means that more thought may be given to the suitability and choice of exhibitions. Trading (and being more than satisfied) with only a handful of clients might indicate that relatively expensive and busy shows are not the

**Businesses**

1. Types

2. Purchasing habits

3. Opinions

4. Exhibition activities

**Exhibitions**

Characteristics:

Benefits:

Drawbacks:

**Individuals**

1. Types

2. Purchasing habits

3. Opinions

4. Exhibition activities

**Exhibitions**

Characteristics:

Benefits:

Drawbacks:

**Looking at your customers: an action checklist**

best medium for promoting yourself to them. Dealing with the public rather than firms may suggest consumer rather than trade events, and vice versa. If customers are all concentrated in one locality where no (or unsuitable) exhibitions are organized, a private show might be arranged with some success. Discussions with customers should also generate details of specific shows that are worth attending and the types of products that ought to be shown there. Filling in 'Looking at your customers: an action checklist' on page 34 may be helpful to you at this time.

## Judging your rivals

It is wise to develop your knowledge of existing and would-be competitors so far as you can. Evaluate them and their goods and services along the same lines that you examined your own firm. Consider their organizations and operations, pencilling in their respective pluses and minuses as you see them. Think about the ins and outs of their products too, dividing them up into benefits and drawbacks where possible. Anything else that can be discovered about them is a bonus and may be of use to you. Refer to Chapter 3: 'Thinking about yourself', page 27, for fuller details.

Investigate and appraise your rivals' attendances at exhibitions and the tactics they have employed at them over the years. See which shows they have exhibited at, what sizes of stands were taken, where those stands were sited, how they were designed and laid out and what goods were on them. It is sensible to know what competing firms are doing in this field, and why. See Chapter 6: 'Choosing exhibitions', page 47, and Chapter 7: 'Designing a stand', page 77, for further information.

Possessing an overall awareness of your rivals and their exhibition activities – probably built up from your dealings with them and by reading and talking about them to other businesses and people in the trade – ought to allow you to press on with your show plans and policies. For example, you may know from attending certain exhibitions that a key, well-established competitor always exhibits at one particular trade event, but not another. Presumably, it has good reasons for doing this and you might be wise to follow (or at least seriously consider) its lead, rather than going against it. See 'Judging your rivals: an action checklist' on page 36 for more assistance with this particular task.

## Studying the marketplace

Be conscious of the main characteristics of your market, including its total size and turnover. Know about the leading manufacturers, wholesalers, retailers and others that trade within it, and their approximate market shares.

## EXHIBITIONS

Characteristics:

Pluses:

Minuses:

## RIVALS

**Positive features** | **Negative features**

1. Main features

2. Goods/services

3. Exhibition activities

**Judging your rivals: an action checklist**

| THE MARKET | | EXHIBITIONS |
|---|---|---|
| **Influences** | **Effects** | |
| 1. Political | 1. Good influences | 1. Consumer |
| 2. Economic | 2. Bad influences | 2. Trade |
| 3. Social | 3. Positive effects | 3. Private |
| 4. Demographic | 4. Negative effects | 4. Pros |
| 5. Other | 5. Trends | 5. Cons |
| 1. Size | | |
| 2. Turnover | | |
| 3. Leading players | | |
| 4. Representative associations | | |
| 5. Statutory bodies | | |

**Studying the marketplace: an action checklist**

Be aware of your representative associations and the ways in which they organize and run the industry. Find out about the relevant statutory bodies and how they administer and restrain the activities of those concerns and individuals working within the marketplace. Have a hands-on feel for what is happening and how everyone interacts and conflicts with each other.

Contemplate the many and varied influences upon the market, separating them out into political, economic, social, demographic, technological and other factors, as appropriate. Calculate how they might affect the marketplace, listing whether they are good or bad influences, with positive or negative effects. Make certain that you recognize any market trends, and whether the market is contracting, stagnating or expanding. Try to spot any significant developments and changes before rather than after they occur. Again, know what is taking place around you.

Having a grasp of your marketplace – typically developed over many years of trading in your particular niche – should enable you to think more fully about the possible merits of consumer, trade and private shows. As an example, your highly respected trade association may organize certain exhibitions, offering the best spaces and substantial discounts to its members. See Chapter 6: 'Choosing exhibitions', page 47. Shifting demographic patterns, perhaps with people (and especially your customers) moving from one region to another, might point you towards exhibiting in the north rather than the south, or vice versa. Have a look at 'Studying the marketplace: an action checklist' on page 37 at this stage. You may find it useful.

## Conducting research

Your own background knowledge and experience combined with a trawl of your books and records, and discussions with relevant persons should provide the basic information needed to draw preliminary conclusions about exhibitions and tactics. Nevertheless, there may be some questions which remain partly or even wholly unanswered. It is therefore sensible to carry out additional research to complete your notes so that they will be of greater assistance to you later on when you proceed to choose exhibitions, design your stand and so on. It is these carefully produced notes – which unwise exhibitors gloss over or omit altogether – that help you to make the correct decisions, and become a successful exhibitor.

Many organizations conduct surveys and collate reports and statistics which incorporate information that may be of interest to you. Depending upon your requirements, consider approaching local authorities, general reference and specialist business libraries and chambers of commerce and trade. Also contact your professional or trade body. If you do not know who or where it is refer to *The Directory of British Associations* which lists leading representative bodies in the United Kingdom; published by CBD Research Limited, it is stocked by most libraries. The Government is a key publisher of business data through Her Majesty's Stationery Office, and a guide listing all of its publications is available from Central Statistical Office. See Appendix D: 'Useful contacts', page 135, for the addresses and telephone numbers of relevant organizations.

On those rare occasions when you cannot find out essential information from your own investigations, you may wish to employ a specialist market research agency to accumulate it on your behalf. Get in touch with the trade bodies in this field: the Association of British Market Research Companies, the Association of Market Survey Organisations and the Market Research Society. They are reputable organizations which will supply a list of their members and offer guidance on the do's and don't's of commissioning a market research company. See Chapter 8: 'Using specialists', page 82, and Appendix D: 'Useful contacts', page 135.

## Summary

1. Would-be exhibitors must familiarize themselves with their current and prospective customers, rivals and the marketplace itself. This preparatory work will allow them to:
   - decide whether exhibitions really are right for their firm
   - substantiate and add to their thoughts about the types of show to attend and how to approach them.

2. When looking at customers, it is advisable to find out about:
   - their characteristics
   - their habits and opinions
   - the relationship between the features of the customer base and those of the different types of exhibition.

3. Prospective exhibitors need to judge their rivals too, particularly in terms of:
   - their organizations, operations, products, services – positive and negative features
   - their attendance at exhibitions and the tactics employed at them
   - their reasons for attending some events but not others.

4. Whilst studying the marketplace, it is sensible to discover as much as possible about:
   • the main characteristics, including its total size, turnover and key participants
   • the many and varied influences upon the market
   • how the marketplace affects the choice and approach to exhibitors, and vice versa.

5. Potential exhibitors can conduct further research into their customers, rivals and the marketplace in a variety of ways, including:
   • looking at published materials such as surveys, reports and statistics
   • talking to professional, trade and other bodies
   • employing a specialist market research agency.

# 5 Setting a budget

**H**AVING DECIDED THAT EXHIBITIONS may be a relevant medium for your firm, you need to go on to identify and analyse all of the possible costs that can be involved with attending a show, deciding which ones are likely to be incurred by you if you proceed. Then you can move ahead to estimate your potential expenditure and conclude whether the outlay required is acceptable to you. Only when these tasks have been completed can you set about choosing exhibitions that are appropriate for your firm.

## Identifying costs

At this stage, you should simply be looking to compile a full and complete list of prospective costs, without trying to calculate which will be most significant to you or assessing how much each of them might actually cost. These two difficult tasks follow on afterwards. For convenience, you can group possible expenses together under headings such as the stand, exhibits, staff and promotion. Indirect costs – especially the time and efforts associated with successful exhibiting – ought to be noted down as well.

Start off by writing out stand-associated costs: stand design; space rental; stand construction; furniture such as desks and chairs; telephone installation and usage; stationery including notepads and enquiry forms; flowers; carpets; catering equipment such as coffee-making facilities; display materials and mountings; security and safety items, such as mirrors and fire extinguishers; electricity, gas, compressed air, water and waste installation and usage; cleaning arrangements; insurance; and stand removal. See Chapter 7: 'Designing a stand', page 77, for fuller information.

With regard to exhibits, expenses will be related to: products; product mountings; assembly, testing and packing; technical literature, including specifications; transportation and storage; installation, perhaps incorporating the use of cranes; withdrawal and return of products. Concerning staff, costs may be linked to: briefings and training courses; uniforms and badges; travel, car parking, accommodation and subsistence; usage of existing staff and additional, hired employees, such as interpreters. Refer to Chapter 8: 'Using specialists', page 82 and Chapter 9: 'Having a successful exhibition', page 91, for more details.

Then move on to set down those costs involved with publicizing yourself, your stand and your goods and services to visitors and the outside world. Promotional expenses could be attributed to: advertising, perhaps via direct mail, show catalogues and trade journals; press releases and kits; company literature, such as brochures, catalogues and price lists; entertainment, possibly including invitations to a dinner dance; refreshments such as light snacks; gifts, incorporating pens, pencils, balloons and key fobs. See Chapter 9: 'Having a successful exhibition', page 91 for further data.

Do not forget to jot down any indirect costs that may be involved with exhibiting at a show, and which are often ill-considered. The time devoted to planning an exhibition, finding out about shows, who's who in the industry and so on ought to be thought about. Perhaps that time could have been spent to the detriment of other work; similarly, the efforts of turning ideas into reality, carrying out some activities and overseeing others might be best directed towards different, more lucrative projects. Fill in the first column of 'Estimating Expenditure: an action checklist' on page 46 at this point.

## Analysing costs

Next, you have to consider all of these costs to ascertain which ones are particularly relevant to you and to mull over the likely figures involved with each of them. Of course, the expenses which will be incurred and the total monies that need to be spent are affected by many factors. In particular, much will depend upon the type of stand chosen, the approach adopted and what you can and cannot do for yourself.

Usually, you will choose between a shell scheme and free-build stand. With a shell scheme, you rent one (or more) of a series of standard, box-like units with a ceiling, walls and floor. A sign, strip-lights and spotlights, power points, furniture, carpet tiles, display mountings and other, miscellaneous items may be included within the price, or could be available for additional, set charges. You are simply responsible for personalizing the basic shell and adding individual exhibits and display materials. With a free-build stand, you rent floor space from the show organizer and are wholly responsible for designing and constructing your stand from scratch, subject to the organizer's approval. Refer to Chapter 7: 'Designing a stand', page 77 and Chapter 8: 'Using specialists', page 82.

Obviously, shell schemes are cheaper at about half the total price of designing and building your own stand. These standardized units are quick and easy to assemble and erect with workmanlike, at-hand materials. However, they are sometimes rather nondescript, may be unsuitable for large and bulky exhibits and could be sited on the edges of the exhibition, away from busy gangways. Freebuilds are more expensive, typically involving larger design fees and longer assembly and erection times with specially purchased materials being used. Nevertheless, they offer greater choice and flexibility, with the opportunity to stand out in a crowd and to incorporate unusual ideas and exhibits.

Clearly, your approach to exhibiting will be a contributory factor towards the costs incurred, and your final bill. To begin with, you may choose to adopt a low-key attitude to feel your way forward – taking a shell scheme, personalizing it with items hired from the organizer and so on. Later, with a track record behind you and more exhibitions planned, you could decide to have a free-build stand designed, furniture and display materials and mountings purchased for long-term, regular use and so forth.

Not least, the total bill will depend upon your own experiences and abilities within this field. Working through your list of would-be costs, you may feel that you possess sufficient, in-house expertise to carry out some tasks yourself such as preparing and transporting exhibits, briefing and training staff, advertising, writing press releases and so on. Other prospective exhibitors – without the expertise or unwilling to commit their time and energies to such activities – may bring in outsiders to attend to these tasks. See Chapter 8: 'Using specialists', page 82. Complete the second column of 'Estimating Expenditure: an action checklist' on page 44 now.

## Estimating expenditure

With a clearer idea of the direct and indirect expenses that you may possibly incur under the headings of the stand, exhibits, staff and promotions, you can then set about adding up all of the probable costs of exhibiting in an attempt to reach a total, minimum to maximum figure. Drawing on your own background knowledge, you should be able to sketch out estimates of many costs, perhaps including printing and producing technical literature, brochures, catalogues and price lists, booking hotel accommodation for your staff, advertising in trade journals, purchasing promotional gifts for giveaways and so on.

Other, more specialized areas – stand design, construction and so forth – will require further research, and representative bodies within the industry should be able to offer some guidance with regard to the likely outlay involved. In particular, the Association of Exhibition Organisers and the British Exhibition Contractors Association can advise on stand and related costs, such as the storage and installation of exhibits, advertising in show catalogues and associated entertainments. The Agricultural Show Exhibitors Association, National Exhibitors Association and the Incorporated Society of British Advertisers Limited can provide general, across-the-board assistance.

| Possible costs | Probable costs | Minimum figure | Maximum figure |
|---|---|---|---|
| 1. The stand | | | |
| 2. Exhibits | | | |
| 3. Stall | | | |
| 4. Promotion | | | |
| 5. Indirect cost | | | |
| 6. Other costs | | | |

**Estimating expenditure: an action checklist**

Refer to Chapter 2: 'Who's who at exhibitions', page 6 and Appendix D: 'Useful contacts', page 135.

By obtaining such a wide range of views and opinions from a number of sources, you should be able to piece together low and high estimates for each possible expense and an overall minimum and maximum figure for exhibiting at an event. Not surprisingly, there are huge differences between what can be spent depending upon your intentions. A small, private event held in a local hall or on your own premises will cost very little, if anything, in purely financial terms; a large, independently-designed stand at a major exhibition can cost thousands of pounds. It is useful to find where your own figures fall within these approximate limits.

Whatever your top and bottom figures, you must then decide whether exhibiting at a show is likely to be a worthwhile activity for your firm. Typically, your main aim in attending an exhibition will be to obtain a certain volume and value of new or additional business and clearly you need to weigh up the costs of exhibiting alongside the likelihood of achieving this aim via this medium (and indeed in comparison to other approaches, such as sales visits). Also, the total expenses have to be set alongside other, difficult to measure goals, such as increasing awareness in the market and finding out more about customers and rivals. See Chapter 9: 'Having a successful exhibition', page 91, for fuller information. Fill in the rest of 'Estimating expenditure: an action checklist' on page 44 now. This will help you clarify your thoughts.

## Summary

1. If it is decided that exhibitions are a relevant advertising medium in the circumstances, a budget consequently needs to be set. This involves:
   - identifying possible costs
   - analysing likely costs
   - estimating actual expenditure
   - concluding whether the anticipated outlay is acceptable in this instance.

2. Possible costs can be identified and categorized under various headings. In particular:
   - the stand
   - exhibits
   - staff
   - promotion
   - indirect costs, such as the time and effort involved.

3. Likely costs to be incurred will be affected by many variable factors, most notably:
   • the type of stand chosen
   • the approach adopted
   • the work that can be completed in-house
   • the work that needs to be done externally.

4. Actual expenditure can be estimated by:
   • drawing on existing, background knowledge
   • referring to representative bodies in the industry
   • piecing together low and high estimates for each expense
   • producing overall minimum and maximum figures for exhibiting – and deciding whether it is worthwhile or not.

# 6 Choosing exhibitions

**Y**OU SHOULD NOW GO ON to shortlist the exhibitions that you might attend, contact organizers to learn more about these shows, make choices about which ones are suitable for you, book spaces and draft a timetable leading up to your first planned event. It is at this stage that all of your earlier, background research into your firm, market and budget will prove to be most useful to you. Be ready to refer to any notes made to help you to reach the right decisions in your circumstances.

## Shortlisting exhibitions

To begin with, you need to obtain a list of exhibitions for the coming year, or for a longer period, if possible. Appendix A: 'Exhibitions, 1997', page 105, provides details for this particular year, although you will find that almost all of the named events are held at the same times and venues by the same organizers every year. Refer to Appendix B: 'Exhibition organizers', page 122, for updates if appropriate. Alternatively, you can buy or subscribe on a regular basis to a publication such as *Conferences and Exhibitions Diary* which supplies extensive information in this field. Appendix E: 'Recommended reading', page 137, describes this and other titles in more depth.

Having already concluded whether you should be exhibiting at either consumer and/or trade shows, it should be relatively easy to read carefully through the list to pick out those events which could conceivably be of potential interest to you. Of course, there are many exhibitions to consider and only brief details are provided – usually topic, date, title, venue and organizer – so if in doubt about the relevance of some, add them to your list of 'possibles' for the moment. It is obviously better to investigate one or two more than to risk missing a potentially ideal show.

Taking events in turn, work through your accumulated notes to whittle down your lengthy list to a shortlist of 'probables'. Compare every show alongside your accumulated notes on your firm, products, services and goals; see Chapter 3: 'Thinking about yourself', page 27. Decide which should remain, and which ought to be deleted. As examples, one show may be too early for your production schedules to gear up to meet the increased, consequent demand; another could be too late for your seasonal goods. Perhaps your objective of increasing awareness of your products in the international arena sounds as though it is unlikely to be fulfilled at an exhibition held in the back of beyond.

Next, think about each show in relation to your customers, rivals and marketplace: refer to Chapter 4: 'Recognizing your market', page 33. For example, conclude if the event is likely to be visited by the right persons, whether tradespeople, members of the general public or both, if appropriate. Also think about whether your leading competitors will be there, and if this is a good or bad sign for you. Naturally, you can still only reach tentative conclusions, and if you are uncertain about a particular exhibition it is wise to keep it in your list for subsequent, further analysis.

## Contacting organizers

Working through your shortlist, you must get in touch with the organizers of each of the events to ask for further information. Not surprisingly, the material sent to you will vary, depending upon whether the organizer is small or large, professional or unprofessional, reputable or disreputable and so on. Hopefully, you should receive a sales brochure, floor plan, booking form and details of the organizer's rules and regulations. It is also sensible to request previous exhibition catalogues, if any are still available. This material and your existing notes will consequently enable you to select the best exhibitions for your situation.

The sales brochure is usually a glossy publication which hypes up the show as best as it can. Although it should be read with a jaundiced eye and a suspicious mind, it does contain some useful information (albeit requiring verification). Typically, it will supply general details about the sponsor, the organizer and its services, the venue, the purpose of the exhibition, show dates and opening hours, the numbers and types of exhibitors and visitors at earlier events and those who are expected on the following occasion. An example of a sales brochure is reproduced on pages 58 to 64.

A large and reputable organizer will provide would-be exhibitors with a copy of the ABC 'Certificate of Attendance' (see pages 12 to 15) as issued by the Audit Bureau of Circulations Limited, see Chapter 2: 'Who's who at exhibitions', page 6. It gives you detailed and independently audited data about the attendance at the last show, which is both helpful and reliable. It does not mean that this will be repeated at the next show, but is a relatively good indicator (and is certainly better than unaudited, hollow claims).

The floor plan, which may need to be requested before it is made available, sets out the scale of the show, the sizes and locations of the stands that are available plus information about the exhibitors who have already booked sites, and their positions. It is wise to check that the exhibitors listed have made firm bookings rather than provisional reservations only, which do not guarantee that they will definitely attend, especially in recessionary times. An example of a floor – or 'hall' – plan is laid out on page 65.

You will be supplied with a booking form. Normally, this gives further, brief data about the show, the venue, dates and times, the types of stand available as well as details of how and when to apply. Your attention will (or should) also be drawn to the contractual obligations which come into effect once the form is completed, signed and returned to the organizer with the appropriate deposit. A booking – or 'space application' – form is reproduced on pages 66 to 68.

The organizer's rules and regulations list the terms and conditions of the contract that apply between the exhibition organizer and the exhibitor on payment and acceptance of the deposit. It covers such topics as the respective rights and responsibilities of the two parties along with specific information on areas such as payments of fees, cancellations, withdrawals and so on. These details – typically set out in microscopic, easy-to-overlook print need to be read in their entirety, by you *and* a solicitor with experience in this field. An example of an organizer's rules and regulations is set out on pages 69 to 74.

Do ask for show catalogues from earlier events and it is probable that one or two will be forwarded to you in due course. These will encompass much of the information previously set out in the sales brochure and other material, and more besides. Typically, it will provide you with fuller details of the sponsor, organizer, venue, exhibitors, visitors and the exhibition industry in general. Peruse it from cover to cover. It is a worthwhile read, conveying a real feel for the event.

## Making choices

Armed with your original notes, organizers' material and being ready to seek advice from other organizations and people as and when necessary, you are now in a position to choose between the various events on your shortlist. You may perhaps wish to nominate one exhibition that you will work towards, with others pencilled in for later on, if all goes well at this first show, see Chapter 9: 'Having a successful exhibition', page 91. Picking out each event in sequence, you need to consider the event itself, the organizer, the venue and the likely exhibitors and visitors in some depth.

Start off by contemplating the show itself. You can probably think of many questions that need to be answered, such as what is its size and status in the field? You may not wish your small, specialist firm to be swallowed up in a huge, sprawling event nor to be associated with an exhibition that gives the impression of being a shoddy, fly-by-night operation. What is its range? You need to know if it is local, regional, national or international in nature, and whether this suits you. If you are aiming to appeal to overseas buyers, you will want to select international events where 20 per cent or more of the visitors are from abroad. Some shows simply have the prefix 'International' attached to their title to puff up a parochial, second-rate event.

Is it a new or well-established show? Should it be new, you have to be certain that a genuine demand exists and that it has not been set up just to promote a venue, or whatever. Discover if it is replacing another event and whether that one failed. If this is the case, find out how the situation has changed or what is different about this exhibition to make it a success. Should it be a well-established event, check how long it has run for. Long-running shows tend to be better choices for new exhibitors as errors have been rectified, everyone knows what they are doing and so on. What competing shows exist? Be wary of attending an event which is close in time or location to another, possibly set up by a rival organizer trying to draw away custom. Usually, exhibitors and visitors split in two, with both exhibitions being less successful than they might otherwise have been.

Next, turn your sights to the organizer, whether this is a trade association, professional exhibition organizer or whoever. Again, you will find that certain queries spring to mind, of which two are most pressing. First: Is is reputable? Not surprisingly, you need to convince yourself that it is not going to take your money and disappear without staging the event. Check its reputation in the trade, how long it has been operating for, what other shows it arranges and whether it belongs to the Association of Exhibition Organizers and/or other representative bodies; refer to Chapter 2: 'Who's who at exhibitions', page 6. Do be especially wary of becoming involved with new, small organizers setting up one-off, solitary events. Some are perfectly respectable, but others have a habit of coming and going under different names, pocketing deposits at every twist and turn.

Second: Is it capable? Equally important, you want to feel confident that it will not only stage the exhibition, but do it well, drawing in the right kinds and numbers of exhibitors and visitors. Obviously, experienced trade associations and well-known exhibition organizers have built up years of know-how and expertise, although past achievements do not necessarily guarantee future success, especially in recessionary times. Even the best organizers can make mistakes and misjudgements, consequently experiencing failure. Find out as much as you can about its plans for the show, with particular emphasis on how it intends to attract exhibitors and promote the event to the desired audience.

Moving on, consider the venue, which many new exhibitors overlook until they arrive prior to the show and find it to be totally unsuitable. Several questions need to be posed and answered satisfactorily: Is it easily reached? You need to be sure that both exhibitors and visitors can get to the site conveniently and on time, so check its proximity to good roads, parking facilities and transport networks, whether buses, trains or planes. Is it large enough? You also want to be certain that the venue is sufficiently spacious for the anticipated numbers to congregate in a relaxed and comfortable atmosphere without being so big that it seems half-empty all of the time, which can cast a downbeat mood on the proceedings.

Is it well structured for exhibitors? Take time to contemplate the large and bulky items that you might show at the event. Decide whether you can deliver, unload and place them on display without difficulty. Investigate access arrangements, lengths and widths, ceiling heights and strengths, possible obstructions and so on. See if there is adequate, controllable light and services such as electricity, gas, water and so forth: refer to Chapter 7: 'Designing a stand', page 77. Is it well laid-out for visitors? Discover if they can walk around it easily, reaching the stands they want to visit and whether restaurant, toilet and other facilities are close at hand.

Then consider the other organizations and individuals who may exhibit at the show. Ascertain the answers to two specific questions: How many exhibitors shall be there? Clearly, you want to see a satisfactory number have been booked so that the exhibition is staged. An adequate quantity must be present so that visitors are drawn to it. What types of exhibitor will be at the event? You have to be sure that the mix of exhibitors is appropriate too. As an example, a show which is designed to attract trade and public visitors in equal numbers should perhaps have exhibitors who will deal with fellow businesses *and* direct with the general public as well.

Last – but most definitely not least – turn your attention towards the visitors who are expected to come to the event. Two key queries will be most prominent in your mind: How many visitors will attend the show? Of greater significance, what types of visitor shall come along to the exhibition? You need to feel confident that both the quantity *and* the quality of the potential visitors are comparable with your own target audience. Do not be swayed into picking events that promise huge numbers of visitors. Unless they are current or prospective customers, they are largely irrelevant to you.

All of these questions – and you can probably add more which are as relevant to you – do need to be answered fully and accurately before you can even think about booking space at any event. Of course, some organizers are scrupulously honest professionals and the material submitted to you is comprehensive and correct, as with the ABC form. Others are untrustworthy, and the information provided is a mixture of hyped-up and deceitful nonsense. Unfortunately, it is sometimes difficult to distinguish reputable organizers from disreputable ones. Therefore, it is always sensible to obtain an extensive and substantiating answer from second and other sources for every question raised.

Contact anyone and everyone who you can think of that might help you by supplying independent and reliable advice and guidance. Get in touch with each of the representative and other bodies involved in the exhibition industry for their views and opinions. In particular, the Association of Exhibition Organisers may offer especially useful assistance concerning organizers, as might the British Exhibition Venues Association with regard to venues. Talk to the Audit Bureau of Circulations Limited about visitors. Consider joining the Agricultural Show Exhibitors Association and/or the National Exhibitors Association to benefit from their help on all aspects of exhibiting. Contemplate employing Exhibition Surveys Limited to conduct a full evaluation. See Chapter 2: 'Who's who at exhibitions', page 6 and Chapter 8: 'Using specialists', page 82.

Perhaps most important of all, chat to exhibitors at the last show and to those who plan to attend the next one. Find out about them and their thoughts on the exhibition, the organizer and so on. Did they match your expectations? Will you exhibit again? If not, why not? Similarly, speak to any visitors who have been to the show, and discover what they have to say about it. Was the venue easy to find? Was there a relaxed atmosphere? Of crucial significance, go out on the road yourself. Visit as many events as you can. See them in action, judge the organizer, appraise the venue and so forth for yourself. Build up your hands-on experience. Know what you are doing before going any further on.

## Booking space

Continuing with your slow but steady, step-by-step approach, you will now want to progress to focus on one initial exhibition, deciding which type of stand you want as well as its size and position before returning your booking form with a deposit. Other potentially suitable shows which are due to be staged thereafter can be pencilled in, with firm bookings being made when – or if – this first exhibition helps you to achieve your goals; refer to Chapter 9: 'Having a successful exhibition', page 91.

You will already have found out about the types of stand that are available and have thought about their pros and cons when you contemplated budgetary considerations earlier on. See Chapter 5: 'Setting a budget', page 41. Whether you favour a shell scheme or an independently designed stand, it is now time to select which one is right for you. If in doubt, refer to those notes again. Perhaps your goal of maintaining your status as the premier manufacturer in your trade might tip the balance towards a unique, designed stand rather than the standardized, shell scheme format. Alternatively, a limited budget may nudge you towards booking a basic shell, albeit with the intention of personalizing it so far as you can. Refer to Chapter 7: 'Designing a stand', page 77.

Selecting the right size and site largely depends upon your specific situation. The dimensions and weight of your goods may mean that a larger stand is needed, whilst various areas could be out of bounds because these items cannot be manoeuvred and placed there safely. If you are trying to appeal to, and expect to have to accommodate, a large number and variety of visitors, you will want to take a big stand where you can be seen by passers-by – perhaps near to the entrance, main gangways and wherever people tend to flow and/or congregate. Steer clear of obstructions, secondary routes and dead-ends unless you expect to meet a small number of hand-picked, personally invited customers who know where to find you and will relish the relatively peaceful environment.

As a general rule of thumb, you will probably not want to draw your customers' attention to your direct rivals by being next to or opposite their stands. However, some newly established, small firms base themselves close to a huge competitor in an attempt to siphon off customers who are milling about, waiting to be seen by busy staff. Such a brazen policy can be successful, assuming the small exhibitor approaches the job in a professional manner. See Chapter 9: 'Having a successful exhibition', page 91.

Some sites may be of limited or even no interest to you if you are operating within a budget, as many exhibitors are. Other positions could be unavailable to you because they have already been booked by fellow-exhibitors. It is not unusual for exhibiting firms to reserve space for the next show as soon as the current one has ended, even if it is planned for three to four years' time. Realistically, your choices – of type, size and site – are always restricted for one reason or another and you should be prepared to be flexible, working within your constraints.

Having settled upon the type, size and site of the stand that you require, you need to fill in and return the booking form with your deposit. Prior to doing this though, do scrutinize the organizer's rules and regulations again. Study each clause in turn, making sure that you understand and approve of all of them. Then take legal advice to clarify and confirm your thoughts and opinions. To all intents and purposes, you are about to enter a legally binding contract and should treat it with due respect, in the same serious manner that you would approach signing any legal document. To take it lightly would be an error of judgement that could prove to be an expensive mistake.

There are numerous, identifiable areas of concern which you can look for. Pose several questions as you read through the clauses. What payments am I committed to make, and when? Usually, you will have to send a 10 per cent deposit with your completed form, with staggered payments spread out perhaps at quarterly intervals up to the show. Try to avoid paying out too much too soon, to maintain your cash flow and to reduce the risks of substantial losses in the event of unforeseen circumstances. Also, check to see what can happen if you are late with a payment – sadly, it is not uncommon to discover you are liable to have your booking cancelled, stand re-sold, monies retained and any remaining balance demanded. Not surprisingly, you will want to avoid exposing yourself to such a scenario.

What changes can the organizer make with regard to the event? Often, you will find that it is legally entitled to alter anything in certain, exceptional situations – from the scope and layout of the show down to the size and position of your individual stand. Clearly, this is not unreasonable as the organizer should be entitled to the final say on how its exhibition is run. Nevertheless, you ought to try to ensure that if changes occur, you retain the right to withdraw and to receive a refund of monies paid, perhaps depending on the extent and effects of the amendments.

What happens if you want to withdraw from the show? Some organizers will demand that you pay the full cost of the space booked before they will release you from your contract with them. You may feel that this is unfair, especially if you give notice in good time, and should therefore seek to have a sliding scale of charges incorporated into the rules and regulations – such as 10 per cent with six months' notice, 25 per cent with three months' notice and so on.

What happens if the exhibition is postponed or cancelled? Hopefully, this will not affect you, although it is unfortunately not an uncommon occurrence. Should it be postponed, you must attempt to make certain that you can pull out of your agreement and retrieve any monies handed over to the organizer to date. Similarly, if it is cancelled, you ought to be looking for a full refund, and indeed compensation for your time, efforts and expenses so far (although this is unlikely to be an achievable aim).

Does the organizer disclaim responsibility for any damages or losses, whenever and howsoever caused? This is a relatively common clause inserted into most if not all of the rules and regulations drawn up by exhibition organizers, and is not wholly unreasonable (although you may wish to try to limit the overall breadth of such a disclaimer). If it is included in your organizer's terms and conditions, you are advised to take out appropriate insurance to protect yourself against damages or losses. Refer to Chapter 9: 'Having a successful exhibition', page 91.

If you or your solicitor come across clauses that you are unhappy with, do not hesitate to haggle over them, seeking their removal or amendments, as relevant. Whatever may be stated in public, these rules and regulations are not cast in stone and many organizers will be ready to negotiate to a certain degree rather than risk losing a prospective exhibitor (and his or her money). As a last resort though, be prepared to walk away from a show rather than committing yourself to a contract that is not in your interests, and might even be detrimental to you. Only sign and return the form and deposit when you are totally satisfied with the agreement.

## Drafting a timetable

Your next step is to note down a list of activities which have to be carried out up to and beyond your first show, followed by the dates by which they must be completed. You need to make absolutely sure that everything is ready and in place before the doors open to visitors. See Chapter 9: 'Having a successful exhibition', page 91. Sketch out all of the tasks which have to be attended to, perhaps grouping them together under the loose (and often interchangeable) headings of the stand, exhibits, staff, promotional and other activities.

With regard to your stand, you will have to do most, if not all, of the following: pick a theme; select contents; tackle presentation; compose a brief for a designer; commission a designer, working to your (amended) brief; submit your stand design to the organizer for approval; alter the stand design, if necessary; employ a contractor to build the stand; order workers' passes from the organizer; supervise erection of the stand; and arrange for the stand to be dismantled and removed after the event. You may be able to add some more tasks which are fitting in your situation, and others could arise as you proceed. In particular, refer to Chapter 7: 'Designing a stand', page 77 and Chapter 8: 'Using specialists', page 82.

Concerning the exhibits, you shall need to carry out these actions, and probably in this (or a very similar) order: prepare relevant, existing and new products for display; examine and test goods for faults; gather up technical literature about the products; transport goods to the contractor or exhibition, as appropriate; arrange for the products to be lifted into place, assembled and installed on the stand, under supervision; and attend to the removal and return of the goods after the show. Again, other activities may be identified now, or at a later date. See Chapter 7: 'Designing a stand', page 77, and Chapter 8: 'Using specialists', page 82, for fuller details.

Turning to the all-important topic of staff, various duties must be overseen, some of vital significance, others apparently mundane. These will include; appointing a stand manager (if not you); selecting the right numbers and types of staff; drawing up a rota; administering a briefing; arranging training; measuring up for uniforms, if appropriate; ordering badges and passes from the organizer; booking accommodation; making travel arrangements; ordering car park tickets; and setting up a debriefing. More tasks will possibly unfold as you set about your workload. Refer to Chapter 9: 'Having a successful exhibition', page 91.

Going on to promotional activities, you should take the following steps, probably in this sequence: compile a prospects list; arrange direct mail shots to customers; submit an entry to the show catalogue, with accompanying advertisement, if relevant; write press releases and complete press kits for distribution; obtain sales literature about yourself; make entertainment arrangements; order giveaways; attend to general advertising campaigns; arrange more direct mail shots to contacts; and write further press releases for the media. Of course, you may also have your own ideas about worthwhile advertising actions, to add to these. See Chapter 9: 'Having a successful exhibition', page 91.

Looking at a final, catch-all heading, you might incorporate these activities: book electrical, gas, compressed air, water and other services; order telephone service, if relevant; order stationery; attend to refreshments arrangements; ensure stand safety and security; take out necessary insurance; and organize stand cleaning. Numerous additional tasks will also spring to mind here, depending on your specific circumstances. More will crop up at later stages. Refer to Chapter 9: 'Having a successful exhibition', page 91.

In many instances, the exhibition organizer will effectively dictate the dates by which tasks have to be finished. As examples, the proposed stand design and your entry for the catalogue have to be submitted at certain times, exhibits have to be on site so many days before the show begins and so on. Thus, most activities can be rearranged into a logical sequence, in order of dates. You will then find that the remaining actions which need to be taken tend to slot into place. For example, you will perhaps want to start work on your catalogue entry and associated advertisement (if appropriate) a month or so before the delivery date, allowing you time to consult with colleagues and take advice, if relevant. See Chapter 9: 'Having a successful exhibition', page 91. When timetabling activities, you may find it helpful to use the project planner on page 59.

# PROJECT PLANNER

Project:

Number:

Completion:

Date:

| Task | Week beginning | | | | | | | | | | | | |
|---|---|---|---|---|---|---|---|---|---|---|---|---|---|
| | | | | | | | | | | | | | |
| | | | | | | | | | | | | | |
| | | | | | | | | | | | | | |
| | | | | | | | | | | | | | |
| | | | | | | | | | | | | | |
| | | | | | | | | | | | | | |
| | | | | | | | | | | | | | |
| | | | | | | | | | | | | | |
| | | | | | | | | | | | | | |
| | | | | | | | | | | | | | |
| | | | | | | | | | | | | | |
| | | | | | | | | | | | | | |
| | | | | | | | | | | | | | |

Project planner form

# A long tradition of gardening

Last year's GLEE, the International Garden & Leisure Exhibition, was the largest ever held with over 750 exhibiting companies and a record-breaking attendance of over 15,000 buyers; this being achieved in what was widely considered to be a recessionary period!
But this is a trend that GLEE has established - consistent growth over the past ten years in line with the

continued expansion of the UK garden and leisure market - and a trend that is likely to continue as we move into the mid-90's with the full impact of the single European Market. Any company, whether UK based or overseas, involved in the manufacture and supply of garden and leisure products should seriously consider the advantages of exhibiting at GLEE. The show is the shop window for the industry covering all aspects of gardening and one that delivers the buyers from garden centres to high street multiples to the DIY

superstores; three types of retail outlet that account for 80% of the estimated total UK garden product sales of £2,000 million each year.
Analysts forecast that sales will continue to grow during the next decade, pointing to good long term prospects for sustained real growth. Among reasons given are more spending on the home, environment issues, expanding market potential from convenience products aimed at the younger gardener, and the growth of the over-55's market as the early retirement trend continues.

THE VISITORS:
Attendance at GLEE 1991 was: Sunday 5,064, Monday 5,678, Tuesday 5,752. Of these visitors, retailers from garden centres, garden shops and florists

accounted for over one in three visitors. Hardware and DIY Stores accounted for just over 5%, major buyers from Department Stores, Multiple shops and Mail Order companies amounted to just under 5%. Machinery Dealers 2.3%. Wholesalers 10.7 %, Press 1.9% and Overseas Visitors 7.4%.

showed a high level of interest in plants. There was also, however, a high level of interest by the majority of visitors in other product categories, e.g. over a third of all machinery dealers indicated an interest in 'outdoor living' primarily garden furniture and nearly a third of DIY Stores were interested in 'nursery products' primarily plants.

Analysis of product interest categories indicated by visitors, not surprisingly, showed a very high level of interest in the visitors main product area, e.g. virtually all garden machinery dealers indicated an interest in garden machinery and wholesale nurseries

**TRADE SPONSORSHIP:**
GLEE is sponsored by major UK trade associations, including The British Hardware and Housewares Manufacturers Association, The Federation of Garden & Leisure Manufacturers, The Horticultural Trades Association and the Leisure and Outdoor Furniture Association.

# Comprehensive service for exhibitors

Any advice that may be needed, especially for a company exhibiting for the first time can be obtained from the GLEE Sales Office. Their first concern is that exhibiting at GLEE should be as smooth running as possible and they are happy to help with any query that may arise however big or small.

They can advise on position and size of stand, contractors, furniture hire, signwriting, catering arrangements – right through to hotel accommodation and travel arrangements.

## MODULAR SHELL STAND

Many exhibitors find it convenient to make use of the modular shell scheme stands. Complete with walling where appropriate, carpet, fascia and name panel, they are ideal for exhibitors who do not wish to be involved with stand design and construction. Sizes start as small as 9 square metres ( 3m x 3m ) and are particularly suitable for the first time exhibitor.

## PUBLICITY MATERIAL

Each year promotional material including invitation cards that can be personalised, and correspondence stickers are produced and supplied free of charge to exhibitors. They form an essential part of the promotional programme for the exhibitor and GLEE.

## THE GLEE CATALOGUE

Produced in an easy to handle A5 size format, the catalogue contains exhibitor entries, combined with product and trade name indices, ( entries are free of charge to exhibitors ), which act as an invaluable reference for purchases throughout the year. Advertising by exhibitors is also available at competitive rates.

## NEW PRODUCTS AND PACKAGING

The New Product and Packaging Stand at GLEE has gained so much significance over the years that most major companies plan their product launches around the exhibition. The massive stand is purpose designed for easy viewing, enabling buyers to assess all that is new in the industry at a glance. Each exhibit

carries the company's stand number where the product can be discussed in greater depth. For the exhibitor, prestigious GLEE DESIGN AWARDS combined with the Stand offer unrivalled benefits in promotional activity.

### GLEE '91 CATEGORIES OF VISITOR

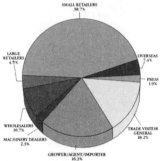

Judged by leading experts in the industry, a product acclaimed at GL⁣ can truly be regarded as the best in the field.

### REGISTRATION AND PRE-REGISTRATION

The computerised registration syste⁣ at GLEE is one of the most sophisticated ever produced for an exhibition.

On completion of a registration car⁣ prior to the show, the visitor will receive an entry badge, advance information on the show, and detail⁣ of new products and special offers available. Additionally a pre-show guide with colour coded plans of th⁣ halls, enables pre-registered buyers plan their visit well in advance, saving valuable time. Visitors unable to pre-register will find entry to the exhibition smoothed by the use of a fast computerised badging system.

**PUBLICITY**
THE GLEE promotional activity is revised annually to achieve maximum publicity for the exhibition and the exhibitors; its aim is to ensure that every potential visitor is fully aware of the importance of GLEE in the home and international calendar. The budget for this world-wide campaign is considerable.
An extensive advertising campaign is carried out in the major garden, hardware, leisure, and ancillary trade press throughout Great Britain and leading European publications, whilst direct mail is targetted at specific retail sectors at home and overseas.
The wide coverage of the press relations programme results in GLEE editorial being published throughout the world. Nearly 200 journalists representing major trade and consumer publications attend GLEE, ensuring considerable publicity for both GLEE and exhibiting companies.

**THE PRESS OFFICE**
The Press Office distributes information concerning GLEE to the trade media throughout the year, commencing immediately after the show with reviews, followed by general exhibition and market data. Leading up to the exhibition, the releases cover the individual exhibitors and particularly any new products that are being launched. To gain maximum publicity from exhibiting at GLEE, exhibitors need to ensure that customers are fully aware of their plans. Promotion assistance is available from the GLEE Press Office, as well as advice on how exhibitors can best promote themselves at the exhibition through the trade magazines.
All the major trade magazines produce extensive editorial previews of GLEE and the exhibitors, and in addition there is a daily newspaper at the show.

**OVERSEAS BUYERS AND JOURNALISTS**
Each year, in conjunction with the DTI, GLEE organises an official group of overseas buyers to visit the show. Different countries are targetted each year, with the buyers representing major retail and wholesale outlets. Overseas buyers have a separate registration point at the show, which leads into an overseas visitor's lounge where interpreters, export/import advice, refreshments and a range of office facilities are available.
In addition, a group of journalists is organised each year, who come from leading garden trade magazines throughout Europe and North America. This results in some excellent editorial coverage for the exhibitor and GLEE.

# The vast range of products on display

**NURSERY PRODUCTS & FLORISTRY**
Plants, Trees & Shrubs,
Seeds & Bulbs,
Cacti & Succulents,
Bonsai,
Cut Flowers,
Landscaping,
Florists Sundries,
Pot Covers & Jardinieres,
Vases & Baskets.

**GARDEN BUILDINGS**
Coldframes,
Conservatories,
Greenhouses,
Sheds,
Summerhouses,
Walling, Fencing & Paving.

**GARDEN CARE PRODUCTS**
Chemicals & Fertilisers,
Compost & Peat,
Non-decorative Plant Pots &

Containers,
Netting & Trellis,
Hosereels & Accessories,
Watering & Irrigation
Equipment,
Wheelbarrows & Rollers.

**GARDEN MACHINERY & TOOLS**
Chain Saws,
Garden Tractors,
Hand Tools,
Lawn Mowers & Equipment,
Power Tools,
Ride-Ons,
Rotary Cultivators.

**OUTDOOR LIVING**
Barbecues & Accessories,
Beach Equipment,
Camping & Caravanning
Equipment,
Furniture for Conservatory,
Garden, Pool & Patio,
Garden Lighting,
Garden Ornaments &
Statues,
Picnic Equipment,
Saunas,
Sports Equipment,
Swimming Pools &
Equipment,
Synthetic Grass & Playing
Surfaces.

**POOLS & PETS**
Fish and Aquaria,
Pets & Cages,
Pet Foods,
Pet Care Products,
Garden Ponds & Water
Plants,
Fountains & Pumps,
Pool Lights.

**GIFTWARE**
Artificial & Dried Flowers,
Christmas Decorations,
Confectionery,
Decorative Pots & Jars,
Hanging Baskets,
Garden Ornaments,
Pot Pourri.

**ANCILLARY PRODUCTS & SERVICES**
Books & Consumer
Magazines,
Computer Equipment &
Software,
Shopfitting & Display
Equipment Signs,
Trade Magazines,
Garden Centre Trollies &
Baskets,
EPOS,
Security Systems &
Equipment,
Heating, Ventilation,
Humidifiers.

FOR FURTHER INFORMATION
OR ANY QUERY, PLEASE CONTACT
CHRIS O'HEA OR STEVE BRYANT
ON 081-390-1601/2211
FAX NO: 081-390-2027.

GLEE IS ORGANISED BY
INTERGARDEN PROMOTIONS LTD
60, CLAREMONT ROAD,
SURBITON, SURREY KT6 4RH.

GLEE 1992 SEPTEMBER 13-15
GLEE 1993 SEPTEMBER 26-28
GLEE 1994 SEPTEMBER 11-13

GLEE
THE HOME
OF BRITISH
GARDENING

# How to get to the NEC

The National Exhibition Centre is a purpose built complex including the exhibition halls, restaurants and banking facilities, railway station, airport, and the Metropole Hotel, and is easily accessible by all means of transport.

By road, there are direct links with a motorway network providing access from all the major cities in the UK, Parking is free for visitors to GLEE, with space for 15,000 vehicles, and a free shuttlebus service links the car parks and the main entrance.

British Rail's Birmingham International Station, alongside the halls, is served by the Inter-City network with travel time from London Euston, being 80 minutes, with Birmingham New Street Station a 10 minute journey. Birmingham International Airport, adjoining the NEC, greatly increases accessibility to the NEC. It provides scheduled service links with 10 UK airports and 19 overseas destinations, and is ideal for day visits to the exhibition. A fast monorail links the airport and the National Exhibition Centre complex.

ACCOMMODATION
The organisers arrange discounted rates at a variety of hotels close to the exhibition. Full details will be sent to all exhibitors on booking.

## THE INTERNATIONAL GARDEN & LEISURE EXHIBITION NATIONAL EXHIBITION CENTRE BIRMINGHAM, ENGLAND 13-15 SEPTEMBER 1992

GLEE is organised by Inter Garden Promotions Ltd., 60 Claremont Road, Surbiton, Surrey KT6 4RH. Telephone: 081-390 1601/2211. Fax 081-390 2027.

NEXT YEAR'S GLEE TAKES PLACE FROM 26-28 SEPTEMBER 1993.

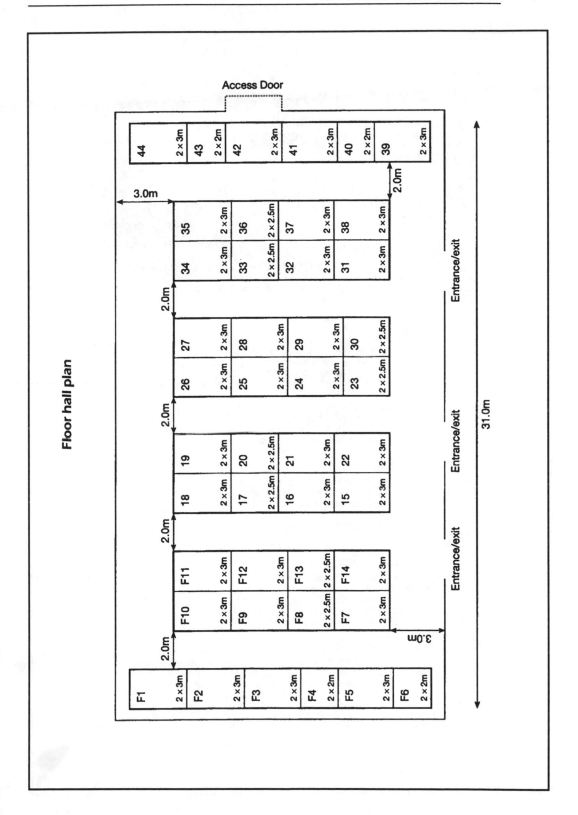

Floor hall plan

## Information and Space Application Form for the
# CHILD AND NURSERY FAIR 1992

Organised by TAS Exhibitions Limited
60 Claremont Road, Surbiton, Surrey KT6 4RH.
Telephone: 081-390 2211/1601
Fax: 081-390 2027

## Venue and Dates

The 1992 Child and Nursery Fair will be held from Sunday 4 October to Tuesday 6 October 1992 inclusive at Earls Court Exhibition Centre, London. Opening times will be 9.30 a.m. to 7.00 p.m. on the Sunday, 9.30 a.m. to 6.00 p.m. on the Monday and 9.30 a.m. to 4.00 p.m. on the Tuesday.

## Space Applications

Companies wishing to exhibit at the 1992 Child and Nursery Fair should complete and return the application form as soon as possible. The application form, together with a cheque for the appropriate deposit including V.A.T., should be made payable to TAS EXHIBITIONS LTD. No applications for space will be considered unless the space application form is completed and signed and accompanied by the appropriate deposit.

Before 1 March 1992 the deposit due is 10% of the total stand rental together with V.A.T. On or after 1 March 1992 but before 1 June 1992 the deposit due is 55% of the stand rental together with V.A.T. On or after 1 June 1992 the full cost of the stand together with V.A.T. must be paid on application.

## Types of Stand

Two main types of stand are available. Firstly Space Only sites where exhibitors arrange for the design and building of their own stands. The cost is £68.00 per square metre. Secondly, Shell Scheme stands, these are constructed from a modular shell scheme by the official contractor. The cost, including space rental is £97.50 per square metre. Full details of both types of stand are in the Rules, regulations and Conditions Note 5a.

## Contractural Obligations

The attention of potential exhibitors is drawn to the fact that once their application has been accepted by the Organisers, or a stand has been allocated to them, then the application will form the basis of a binding contract. Once a site has been chosen a confirmation letter will be sent to the exhibitor, detailing any changes to the original application. This letter will modify the terms of the contract.

## N.B. Space Only Sites

Where more than one exhibitor occupies an island site, the organisers will provide a traditional dividing wall painted white. No charge will be made for this service. The exhibitors contractor will be permitted to use this wall as part of any stand construction and exhibitors should ensure that any specification provided by their contractor does not include provision of this walling. This ensures that all dividing walls conform to a common standard improving the overall appearance of the adjoining stands. Walling will not be provided for perimeter sites and these should be provided by the exhibitors own contractors.

Return this form to
TAS EXHIBITIONS LTD
60 CLAREMONT ROAD, SURBITON
SURREY KT6 4RH
Tel: 081-390 2211  Fax: 081-390 2027

| FOR ORGANISERS USE ONLY |
| --- |
| Deposit Paid ........................................ |
| Date Paid ............................................. |
| Space/Shell  ☐ BPA Member |
| Stand No. ............................................ |
| Width .................. Depth ................ |
| Deductions ......... Area ................... |

# APPLICATION FORM

## CHILD AND NURSERY
## FAIR 1992

Sunday 4 October to Tuesday 6 October 1992
Earls Court Exhibition Centre, London, England

Company Name ...........................................................................................................

Address .......................................................................................................................

.....................................................................................................................................

Telephone: ................................................................... Fax:...........................................

Name of contact responsible for stand ...........................................................................

I/We apply for a stand at the 1992 Child and Nursery Fair.

I/We agree to abide by Rules, Regulations and Conditions overleaf and further agree that a binding contract will exist on acceptance of this application by the Organisers or by allocation of a stand.

I/We require ..................... m² of * space only/* shell scheme (*delete as appropriate - see note 1).

NOTE 1
1992 charges are as follows:

Space Only Stands ..... £68.00 per m²      Shell Stands ................. £97.50 per m².

I/We agree to pay the total sum applicable to this stand, plus V.A.T. at the prevailing rate, in the instalments shown in the Conditions overleaf, not later than the due dates.

I/We enclose a cheque for the appropriate deposit for the stand applied for, together with V.A.T. thereon.

I/We understand that time will be of the essence with regard to all payments as set out in Clause 11 of the Conditions overleaf.

I/We agree the terms of the discount available to members of the Baby Products Association as detailed below:-
Members of the Baby Products Association are entitled to a 10% discount on stands, provided they are fully paid up members of the Association at 1st June 1992.
By agreement, half of the 10% discount is paid direct to the Baby Products Associationt by the Organisers and the eligible exhibitor will be credited with the remaining 5% in accordance with the conditions printed opposite.
To qualify for the discount, payment of the final invoice and any other balance outstanding must be made by 30th June 1992.
The discount will be deducted from the final invoice for eligible exhibitors, previous invoices will be calculated on the full cost of the stand.
No discount is available to exhibitors booking after 1st June 1992.

I/We confirm that our major activity is (tick one box):-
Manufacturer ................................. ☐   Sole Importer/Sole Distributor ........ ☐

## Products to be Exhibited

I/We have ticked below the main types of products to be exhibited on my/our stand.

| | | | |
|---|---|---|---|
| ( 1) Baby Care Products | .......... | ( 2) Baby Clothing | .......... |
| ( 3) Baby Food | .......... | ( 4) Baby Walkers/Bouncers | .......... |
| ( 5) Boys Clothing | .......... | ( 6) Carry Cots | .......... |
| ( 7) Christening Wear | .......... | ( 8) Component and Material Supplies | .......... |
| ( 9) Co-ordinated Bedding | .......... | (10) Cots | .......... |
| (11) Feeding Items | .......... | (12) Girls Clothing | .......... |
| (13) High Chairs | .......... | (14) Mattresses | .......... |
| (15) Nursery Furniture | .......... | (16) Prams & Accessories | .......... |
| (17) Pre School Toys | .......... | (18) Publications | .......... |
| (19) Pushchairs & Accessories | .......... | (20) Safety Products | .......... |
| (21) Soft Toys | .......... | (22) Other (please state) | .......... |
| ..................................... | .......... | ..................................... | .......... |

## Sole Importers/Sole Distributors

This section is to be completed only by exhibitors who are importers or distributors of the goods concerned.
I/We list below all companies whose goods I/We will be exhibiting:-

1   Manufacturers Name ....................................................................................................

    Address ....................................................................................................................

    ....................................................................................................................

2   Manufacturers Name ....................................................................................................

    Address ....................................................................................................................

    ....................................................................................................................

3   Manufacturers Name ....................................................................................................

    Address ....................................................................................................................

    ....................................................................................................................

4   Manufacturers Name ....................................................................................................

    Address ....................................................................................................................

    ....................................................................................................................

5   Manufacturers Name ....................................................................................................

    Address ....................................................................................................................

    ....................................................................................................................

(list further manufacturers on separate sheet if necessary).

**No application for space will be considered unless properly signed and accompanied by the appropriate deposit. Overseas exhibitors should pay by sterling draft on a London clearing bank.**

Signed ............................................................................................ Date..................................

Position ....................................................................................................................

*Note:- If a limited company, this form must be signed by a director of the company, if a firm by a partner and if a sole trader by the proprietor.*

## DEFINITIONS

In the Conditions and in any Rules and Regulations from time to time made by the Management the following expression shall (unless inconsistent with the particular context thereof) have the following meanings:

Exhibition – International Garden and Leisure Exhibition ('GLEE')

Exhibition Days and Hours – Sunday 13 September 1992, Monday 14 September 1992 and Tuesday 15 September 1992 from 9.00 a.m – 6.00 p.m.

Exhibitor – Any person firm company or other body corporate to whom a Stand Licence is granted.

Management – Inter Garden Promotions Limited.

Exhibition Site – National Exhibition Centre.

Premises – That part of the Exhibition Site allocated for the holding of the Exhibition.

Stand Licence – The Licence granted by the Management to an Exhibitor to erect and use a stand on the Premises during the Exhibition Period for the purposes of the Exhibition which licence shall be deemed to be granted on and subject to the Conditions and any Rules and Regulations from time to time in force thereunder.

NEC – The National Exhibition Centre Limited.

NEC Rules and Regulations – All Rules and Regulations made by the NEC concerning the use and occupation of the Premises and Exhibition Site from time to time in force.

Relevant Authorities – NEC the Management all Authorities as defined in the NEC Rules and Regulations and the Electricity Board and Gas Board and the Water Authority as herein defined and their respective servants and agents.

Licence Fee – The fee for a Stand Licence for a stand of the size and type alloted to an Exhibitor and Value Added Tax thereon.

Special Services – All gas, compressed air, electricity, water or other services supplied to any stand and all connections to each stand for the supply of the same and for telephones and the removal of waste (in the case of connections for electricity being such connections up to but not beyond the distribution point or points on each stand).

Special Service Charge – All or any charges for the supply or connection to each stand of any Special Services.

Setting-up Period – 8.00 a.m. Tuesday 8 September to 12.00 noon Saturday 12 September.

Stand Dressing – 12.00 noon Saturday 12 September to 8.00 a.m. Sunday 13 September.

Pulling-down Period – 6.15 p.m. Tuesday 15 September to 4.00 p.m. Thursday 17 September. Or such other periods as the Management may notify Exhibitors as the respective times for the erection and dressing of the respective stands and the dismantling and removal of the same.

Exhibition Period – The Setting Up Period the Exhibition Days and the Pulling Down Period.

## RULES AND REGULATIONS

In these Rules and Regulations words and expressions used shall where appropriate and unless inconsistent in the particular context have the same meanings as are respectively ascribed thereto in the Conditions.

A Each Exhibitor will observe and will procure the observance by his employees agents contractors sub-licencees and invitees of the NEC Rules and Regulations and any directions given by any relevant authority concerning the use and occupation of the Exhibition Site or any part or parts of it. In particular (but without limitation) each Exhibitor will ensure that each of his employees is fully conversant with precautions to be taken against, and procedures to be followed in the event of, fire. The Management will on request supply or make available for inspection copies of the NEC Rules and Regulations.

**Organizer's Conditions, Rules and Regulations**

B Subject thereto and to the intent that in the event of any inconsistency the NEC Rules and Regulations shall override the rules and regulations set out below each Exhibitor will observe and procure the observance by his employees agents contractors sub-licencees and invitees of the following rules and regulations:

1 Each stand shall be used solely for the purposes of the Exhibition.

2 Each Exhibitor will ensure that his stand is open to view and adequately staffed throughout the Opening Hours on Exhibition Days. In the event of failure on the part of any Exhibitor so to do the Management shall be at liberty at the Exhibitor's expense in each case and without being liable for any resultant loss or damage to take all or any reasonable steps to ensure that such stand is so open and staffed.

3 The Management reserves the right to refuse admission to any person without assigning any reason therefor.

4 Each Exhibitor will procure that his stand or other temporary structure erected by him is erected and maintained to reasonable and proper standards of construction having particular regard to the planning fire and other regulations of the relevant authorities and will ensure that all items displayed on or about the stand shall so conform.

5 Each Exhibitor will procure that his stand is properly managed and that he his employees agents contractors sub-licencees and invitees conduct themselves in a proper and unobjectionable manner and no Exhibitor will display or permit to be displayed any offensive or obscene material. The Management reserves the right to expel any person from the Premises who does not so conduct himself and to close any stand which is not so managed or on which such material is displayed or if in the reasonable opinion of the Management he or it is or may become a nuisance or annoyance to the NEC or Management or to other Exhibitors or their respective employees agents contractors sub-licencees or invitees as the case may be.

6 No Exhibitor will place or keep or permit or suffer to be placed or kept on in under or over the Premises or any part thereof any substance which is in the opinion of the Management of a dangerous explosive or objectionable nature.

7 Each Exhibitor shall make good all and any damage to the Exhibition site or the premises suffered or caused by any act or default of himself his employees agents contractors sub-licencees or invitees (damage by risks insured against pursuant to Condition 3(1) only excepted).

8 No Exhibitor will interfere with or make any alterations attachments or additions to the Premises and will not place any unusual load on any beam pillar or other part of the premises or allow any such load to be so placed.

9 No Exhibitor will park on or otherwise obstruct and will ensure that none of his servants or agents shall park on or otherwise obstruct any part of the Exhibition Site save as may be permitted by NEC.

10 Each Exhibitor will take all or any Special Services required for his stand only from NEC. In the event that NEC shall not be able to provide the supplies needed by the Exhibitors only such mode of generation or supply as shall first be approved by NEC or by the Management shall be used. Charges for any Special Services requested by an Exhibitor will be additional to the Licence Fee and such charges must be paid direct to the NEC or their appointed agents. The Management can accept no responsibility in relation to the provision of Special Services.

11 Exhibitors must ensure that all work on the construction, assembly, erection, decoration and dismantling of exhibition stands is carried out by contractors who are either members of The British Exhibition Contractors Association or have been specifically approved by the Organisers. The Organisers reserve the right to stop work on any stand construction and, if necessary, to employ approved contractors at the exhibitor's expense to complete any work on the stand if these conditions are not

complied with.

12 Each Exhibitor will procure that all beverages alcoholic drinks food ice cream sweets confectionery and (except as regards personal requisites) tobacco and other consumable refreshment of any nature whatsoever which are to be consumed on the Premises by themselves and their employees and invitees respectively are obtained from the NEC.

13 Each Exhibitor will only deliver and remove stands and any equipment or fixtures and fittings therefor, exhibits and other goods of whatsoever nature during such reasonable hours as the Management may from time to time notify that Exhibitor. The Management can accept no responsibility therefor.

14 Each Exhibitor will procure the immediate removal from the Premises of all his packing cases packaging material and rubbish or waste of any description and will not store or permit the same to be stored thereon and in the event of any default the Management shall be at liberty to remove the same at the cost of the Exhibitor.

CONDITIONS

1 Payment of Licence Fee

(1) The Licence Fee shall be payable

(a) as to 10% of the Licence Fee for the size and type of stand applied for on making an application for a Stand Licence.

(b) as to 35% of the Licence Fee for the size and type of stand allocated or (in the event that the Stand Licence actually granted shall be for a stand of a different size and/or type from that applied for by the Exhibitor) an amount equal to the outstanding balance of 45% of the Licence Fee for the Stand Licence actually granted on or before 1st December 1991.

(c) as to 30% of the Licence Fee on or before 1 March 1992.

(d) as to the outstanding balance of the Licence Fee on or before 1 June 1992.

(2) In the case of each instalment of the Licence Fee payable as hereinbefore men-

tioned each Exhibitor will pay an amount equal to the Value Added Tax thereon at the appropriate rate

(3) Without prejudice to the provisions of Condition 6 hereof if an Exhibitor shall fail to pay the Licence Fee or any Value Added Tax in respect thereof in accordance with these Conditions then that Exhibitor shall in addition to the sums above specified pay the Management interest at the rate of 1.5% per month on the outstanding balance.

(4) Any Exhibitor resident or incorporated outside the United Kingdom shall make payment of all monies due or to become due under these Conditions by means of a sterling draft drawn on a London Clearing Bank.

(5) If any instalment of the Licence Fee referred to in paragraph (1) of Condition 1 or any Value Added Tax or interest payable under these conditions shall be unpaid for 14 days after the due dates for payment thereof (whether the same shall have been demanded or not) or if any Exhibitor shall fail substantially to observe or fulfil all or any of these Conditions, Rules or Regulations, then the Stand Licence may be determined immediately by the Management. In this case the Management may retain any monies already paid under the Stand Licence and any remaining balance due under the Stand Licence shall immediately become payable by the Exhibitor.

2 Cancellation or Interruption

(1) If by reason or force majeure fire tempest explosions of any kind failure or neglect of anybody supplying electricity power gas or water strikes or workmen labour difficulties or shortage of materials or other cause (whether ejusdem generis or not) beyond the control of the Management and whether occurring before or during the Exhibition Period the Management is prevented or hindered from holding the Exhibition on the Exhibition Days or any of them or the use of the whole or any part of the Premises during the Exhibition Period or any part thereof for or in connection with

the Exhibition is prevented or inhibited then the Management shall be entitled to cancel or suspend the holding of the Exhibition or the use of any part of the Premises for those purposes and in particular (but without limitation) shall be entitled to cancel or suspend any Stand Licence granted to any Exhibitor or make such alterations in the terms thereof as it shall in its absolute discretion think fit.

(2) In the event of cancellation or suspension of the Exhibition or the cancellation or suspension or alteration of any Stand Licence pursuant to paragraph (1) above the Management shall be under no liability to any Exhibitor for any damage or loss which such Exhibitor may sustain in consequence of any such cancellation suspension or alteration.

(3) Such cancellation or suspension shall not affect the liability of any Exhibitor to make any payment of the Licence Fee or any Value Added Tax or interest provided for by these Conditions and the Management shall in its absolute discretion be entitled to retain or recover payment of any such monies.

(4) In the event of the cancellation or suspension of the Exhibition as a whole the Management (but without being liable in any way for any failure so to do) will endeavour to make arrangements for the holding of a similar exhibition.

3 Insurance and Indemnity

(1) The Management will use all reasonable endeavour to procure that the NEC shall insure in the names of the NEC the Management and each Exhibitor and their contractors and such other persons as NEC and the Management may agree (hereinafter called 'the insured') against public liability on the part of the insured or any of them with an indemnity limit of £10,000,000 (or such other limit as NEC and the Management may agree) on any one claim or series of claims arising from any one event and causing death bodily injury illness disease or loss of or damage to property during the Exhibition Period and happening upon the Exhibition Site including the Premises provided always that there shall be excluded from the risks so insured such risks as NEC and the Management may from time to time in their absolute discretion agree including (but without limitation)

(i) employers' liability claims

(ii) in the case of the Management Exhibitors and their respective contractors any liability arising from goods, products or samples supplied sold or distributed

(iii) damage to the Exhibition Site fixtures and fittings caused by fire explosion aircraft riot and civil commotion malicious damage storm and tempest burst pipes flood impact and consequential loss.

(iv) occurrences at the Warwick and Metropole Hotels

(v) property belonging to an individual insured and damaged by an act of that individual insured his employees or contractors

(vi) the use of the premises for activities other than trade exhibitions

(vii) any vehicle licensed for road use or otherwise subject to compulsory insurance.

(2) No Exhibitor will omit or do or cause to be done any act, matter or thing whereby the policy referred to in the preceding sub-paragraph or any material damage or other policies from time to time effected by NEC or the Management shall be rendered void or voidable or whereby any moneys payable thereunder shall be withheld or the amount of any moneys so payable shall be reduced.

(3) Save and subject as aforesaid all public liability insurance all insurance against loss of or damage to the property and effects of Exhibitors and their respective employees agents contractors and invitees or against injury loss or damage suffered by Exhibitors or any agent of or any persons employed by any of them or by their invitees or to their respective property and effects or against consequential loss suffered by them or any of them shall be the responsibility of the Exhibitor or other persons affected and each Exhibitor shall indemnify and save harmless the Management against all claims which may be made against the

Management in respect of any such matter save only injury loss or damage caused by the act default or negligence of the Management or its employees or agents and in respect of any material damage to the Premises (including buildings and Landlord's fixtures and fittings thereon) and any consequential loss to NEC or any other person or body resulting from any act or default of such Exhibitor or any of his employees agents contractors or invitees.

4 Rules and Regulations
Each Exhibitor shall during the Exhibition Period observe and perform the Rules and Regulations hereinbefore set out and any further or amended or modified Rules and regulations which the Management shall from time to time during the Exhibition Period think fit to impose including all Rules and Regulations concerning the use and occupation of the Premises and the Exhibition Site for the time being imposed by the NEC.

5 Overseas National Stands
Organisers of Overseas National Stands are responsible for ensuring that all Exhibitors on their stands are fully aware of and agree to abide by all the current Rules and Regulations and Conditions.

6 Bankruptcy
If an Exhibitor (being an individual) shall become bankrupt or (being a Company) shall enter into liquidation whether compulsory or voluntary (save for the purpose of amalgamation or reconstruction of a solvent Company) or if a Receiver shall be appointed of its undertaking or if an Exhibitor shall enter into an arrangement or composition for the benefit of that Exhibitor's creditors or shall suffer any distress or execution to be levied on that Exhibitor's goods then and in any such case it shall be lawful for the Management forthwith to give Notice determining his or its Stand Licence. Payments made hereunder shall be absolutely forfeited to the Management but without prejudice to any of the

Management's rights or remedies in respect of such default breach or omission.

7 Withdrawal of Exhibitors
(i) Once an application for a Stand Licence has been accepted in writing by the Management and a site has been allocated, the Exhibitor cannot be released from his contractual obligations. If in exceptional circumstances (force majeure etc.), release from the Stand Licence is granted by the Management then the following scale of cancellation charges will apply:
Cancellation before 1 March 1992. 10% of total cost of stand together with V.A.T. thereon.
Cancellation on or after 1 March 1992, but before 1 June 1992. 45% of total cost of stand together with V.A.T. thereon.
Cancellation on or after I June 1992 but more than 60 days before the opening of the Exhibition. 75% of total cost of the stand together with V.A.T. thereon.
Cancellation within 60 days of the opening of the Exhibition. 100% of the total cost of the stand together with V.A.T. thereon.
(ii) The above conditions and cancellation charges will also apply pro-rata to any reduction in stand size requested by an Exhibitor once a stand has been allocated.

8 Variation of Opening Hours
The Management reserves the right in its absolute discretion to alter or vary the Opening Hours.

9 Literature
The Management will use all reasonable care in the preparation of any literature issued by it in connection with the Exhibition but it will not be responsible for any error therein contained and no such error shall entitle an Exhibitor to any remedy whether by way of rescision of the Licence or damages or otherwise howsoever.

10 Assignment
The benefit of a Stand Licence is personal to the Exhibitor to whom it is granted and no Exhibitor shall or shall purport to assign

deal with or otherwise dispose in any manner whatsoever with his interest thereunder
or any part thereof.

11 Promotional Events
In order that attendance by buyers and/or
press will not be adversely affected each
exhibitor agrees that he will not organise or
participate in any form of event or promotional activity, within 25 miles of the NEC,
during the open hours of the exhibition
unless that event or activity takes place
within the premises.

12 Variation of Conditions
Only the Management has authority to vary
all or any of the above Conditions or alter all
or any of the Rules and Regulations made
by the Management and from time to time
in force.

## Summary

1. Choosing exhibitions is a task which needs to be approached carefully. It involves:
   - shortlisting exhibitions
   - contacting organizers
   - making choices
   - booking spaces
   - drafting a timetable.

2. Exhibitions can be shortlisted by:
   - obtaining a list of exhibitions for the coming year or longer
   - selecting those of potential interest
   - comparing these 'possibles' with the firm's products, services and goals – and retaining or deleting them as appropriate
   - studying the remaining 'possibles' in relation to customers, competitors and the marketplace – consequently whittling down to a shortlist of 'probables'.

3. Organizers of shortlisted exhibitions should be contacted for further information about their events. Ask for:
   - sales brochures
   - Certificate of Attendance forms
   - floor plans
   - booking forms
   - rules and regulations
   - previous exhibition catalogues.

4. Choices need to be made by taking each shortlisted exhibition in sequence and studying:
   - the event itself
   - the organizer
   - the venue
   - the likely exhibitors
   - the likely visitors.

5. Focusing on the first exhibition to be attended, space needs to be booked well in advance. This means:
   - selecting the right type of stand
   - picking an appropriate size of stand
   - choosing the correct position for the stand
   - studying the rules and regulations to ensure they are acceptable
   - returning the completed booking form with a deposit.

6. A timetable needs to be drafted up to and beyond the first show, with activities scheduled in relation to:
   - the stand
   - exhibits
   - staff
   - promotions
   - miscellaneous matters.

# 7 Designing a stand

**W**HATEVER THE TYPE, size and position of stand planned, you should now spend some time considering its design. You need to contemplate its appearance, select contents and compose a brief for whoever is to be employed to turn your thoughts into reality. Realistically, the design and subsequent construction of your stand will be carried out by specialists in this field – typically a freelance designer and a contractor nominated by the exhibition organizer – but you ought to have a broad idea of what you want before approaching them for professional help and guidance.

## Contemplating appearance

You must not try to design your exhibition stand yourself, unless you possess hands-on knowledge and genuine expertise in this area. Even the personalization of a shell unit should be referred to an experienced stand designer, or at least be carried out following his or her extensive advice and suggestions. Too many exhibitors adopt a DIY approach because they naively believe that they have a flair for colour co-ordination, can stack a pile of goods in an imaginative way and (not least) will save money. As a consequence, they 'design' an amateurish hotch-potch of a stand which conveys a poor impression and leaves customers unmoved or alienated. Take an administrative rather than an artistic role, deciding what you would like prior to going to an expert. See Chapter 8: 'Using specialists', page 82.

Your stand should perform several functions, and will do if it is designed properly. It ought to create and put across the desired image of your firm. Be clear about what message you want to convey to visitors and customers. It may be that you wish to tell them you are a wholesaler who can supply any and every item they could conceivably need to run and maintain their business equipment without interruption. Alternatively, you might want to confirm that you are a well-established, leading manufacturer in your particular industry. Think how these (and other images) may be conveyed to the outside world, perhaps by the difficult task of displaying every product stocked or through having a glossy stand decked out in your firm's familiar logo and colours.

Your stand also needs to be attractive enough to draw visitors to it and to make them come and talk to staff, pick up a brochure or whatever. Again, consider what can be done to achieve this aim: have some ideas to put to the designer. Perhaps a banner or a flag showing your logo and colours may be attached to the top of your stand to attract people from afar. Similarly, a matching fascia might tug at those visitors who are a little closer to you. When walking by, an out-of-reach new product, an intriguing photograph, a heard but not seen audio-visual display, even the possibility of a cup of tea and a sit-down could entice them. Your staff can do much to attract them too. Refer to Chapter 9: 'Having a successful exhibition', page 91.

The stand is also a working environment, where customers and staff meet to establish contact, build a rapport, place and take orders and so forth. This should never be overlooked and everything possible ought to be done to ensure that they can do this in a comfortable and convenient manner. Contemplate and prepare some suggestions for the designer. You may feel an office area with desks and chairs is needed, perhaps closed off if confidential deals are to be made. You could decide that your staff want product samples, information files and technical and promotional literature at hand to support them. Customers will want to feel relaxed and at ease in a place which is neither too brightly lit, hot, cold nor loud.

With many thoughts in your head, you may begin to believe that you and/or your colleagues are enormously creative and feel that you are itching to design the stand yourself. Resist this understandable temptation, however powerful it is. Unless you are well qualified, you are no more likely to be able to create a winning stand than you are to design a car that drives itself. This is a highly complex, specialized field, too often tackled by amateurs with half-baked ideas and unlimited confidence – and it invariably ends with disastrous consequences. Stick to what you do best, and employ others to carry out remaining work on your behalf.

## Selecting contents

Although your chosen designer will be responsible for overall display tactics, you must obviously select those products that should be exhibited on the stand. In many instances, this will be a relatively straightforward choice: a new range of goods is being launched onto the market, a set of products has been refined and repackaged for a different market, seasonal goods are available for sale for a limited period only and so on. Your selection will simply reflect and enhance the activities and goals of your firm, whether to sell a certain volume or value of goods in a given region or time, or whatever.

On other occasions, your choice may be less obvious. Some products might be too large and heavy to display at this venue (although you should therefore question whether this is the right event for you). Various goods may not be ready to be displayed, demonstrated and examined by customers, which might suggest you are not yet in a position to exhibit. You could wish to show all of your stock to prove you are the best wholesaler in the region, but only have a limited and insufficient amount of space available to do this. You may want to convey the impression that you are the market leader and just do not know which products will help to strengthen this image.

In these and similar situations you are faced with a difficult dilemma, and need to think carefully about what to do. Even if they are big and cumbersome, try to display the items that you want to sell though this may involve taking a larger stand. Photographs, illustrations and the like do have a role to play on a stand but there is little point in attending an exhibition to show a picture of a product that could just as easily be seen in a brochure or catalogue. Always make certain that displayed goods can be handled and tested, and will perform as expected. Prototypes and models are poor replacements. If you are unable to decide between products, you may wish to pick a blend of your best-sellers and those goods that cannot be promoted effectively by other means, perhaps because they are too big to be loaded into a sales agent's car and so on.

Visual display items can be incorporated on the stand as well, to back up your exhibits. Photographs, diagrams and illustrations with clear and concise captions may be placed on the inside or outside of your unit, on ceilings, walls or even floors. They could possibly show different parts of a product and how they are assembled together or might illustrate how your services are carried out on a step-by-step basis. It is sensible to have these materials produced especially for the show. As an example, a photograph in a catalogue may not be of a sufficiently high quality when blown up to the size required for an exhibition stand. Talk to the Association of Illustrators, British Institute of Professional Photography, British Printing Industries Federation, and the Society of Typographic Designers for advice. See Appendix D: 'Useful contacts', page 135.

Audio-visual displays may be a beneficial addition to your stand too, whether in the form of a slide show, film or video presentation. Think about whether these will substantiate and further your message, help to promote your goods and services and maintain a quality working environment. Sometimes, you may feel that the distraction from face-to-face contact, the noise levels and the time and effort involved with setting up and running such displays are not worthwhile. Also, the organizer's rules and regulations often limit or even forbid these activities if they are a nuisance to your neighbours, possibly by causing crowds to build up and block gangways. Gather your thoughts and ideas together before chatting about them to a designer.

## Composing a brief

Knowing roughly what you want, you now need to compile a brief for whoever will have to translate your ideas into a finished product, usually a freelance designer, followed by an on-site contractor: see Chapter 8: 'Using specialists', page 82. The brief must incorporate all of the information required by the designer to design an appropriate stand for you. Clearly, the details needed will vary according to individual circumstances but might be grouped under the various and familiar headings of the firm, the market, the show and the stand.

With regard to your firm, you may wish to provide background information about its organization, especially its marketing and advertising policies, the desired image and a who's who of contact names and responsibilities; products and services, with descriptions and comments on good and bad features; objectives, outlining how attending this event will help to achieve them; and budget, with a breakdown of how monies are allocated. Concerning the market, you could decide to put down data about your: customers, describing their characteristics and habits; rivals, with special emphasis on those exhibiting at the show; and marketplace, explaining your position within it. Refer to Chapter 3: 'Thinking about yourself', page 27, Chapter 4: 'Recognizing your market', page 33 and Chapter 5: 'Setting a budget', page 41.

In relation to the show, you ought to cover: the event itself with dates, opening times and reasons for its selection; the venue, including a floor plan, and comments on its positive and negative aspects and flow patterns; the organizer, with a copy of their rules and regulations; exhibitors, particularly those close to and/or in direct competition with your firm; and visitors, with notes on their numbers and types. For the stand, you should explain its: type, whether a shell scheme or free-build unit; size, incorporating its height, width and depth; site, with its stand number, key features and proximity to other units and facilities, such as restaurants and toilets. See Chapter 6: 'Choosing exhibitions', page 47.

In addition, you must set down: the message you wish your stand to convey to the outside world, such as being the biggest stockist or leading manufacturer in the trade; thoughts about its appearance, perhaps incorporating banners and flags; ideas about its working environment, possibly including an office area, desks, chairs and so forth; exhibit details, with data about their numbers, dimensions, weights, pros, cons, special features and so on; display material details, incorporating photographs, drawings and so forth; audio-visual suggestions, such as videos; staff names, numbers, positions, roles and responsibilities whilst on the stand. Refer to Chapter 9: 'Having a successful exhibition', page 91.

Hopefully, you will sketch out all of this information now – for clarification of your own intentions as much as anything else – and have it to hand when you go out to seek and commission a stand designer. Naturally, he or she will confirm the precise details that are required from you and the order and layout in which they should be presented for his or her use. You can then attend to this task in a rapid and efficient manner.

## Summary

1. Designing a successful exhibition stand incorporates three key steps:
   - contemplating its appearance
   - selecting its contents
   - composing a brief for the designer and contractor.

2. The stand should:
   - create the desired image of the firm
   - be attractive enough to draw visitors to it
   - provide a satisfactory sales and working environment
   - *never* be self-designed – this is a highly specialized task.

3. The contents of an exhibition stand could incorporate:
   - products that can be displayed and sold effectively in an exhibition environment
   - visual display items, such as photographs, diagrams and illustrations
   - audio-visual displays, like slide shows, films or video presentations.

4. The brief for the designer and contractor may be detailed under the headings of:
   - the firm
   - the market
   - the show
   - the stand
   - miscellaneous matters.

# 8 Using specialists

HAVING THOUGHT CAREFULLY about the design of your stand and possessing numerous ideas which you would like to see incorporated within the finished product, you can proceed to commission a designer and employ a contractor to design and build the stand on your behalf. It is vitally important that you take special care when choosing and consequently using specialists because you are very dependent upon them for your success.

## Commissioning a designer

You can obtain design services from one of several sources, typically a freelance designer, design house or a contractor. A freelance designer who has managed to survive and prosper through recessionary times is likely to be imaginative, helpful and should have a broad-based knowledge of and expertise in various aspects of exhibition stand design and construction techniques. However, a small-business person may lack a depth of experience in certain, key areas and with limited resources might not be able to take his or her stand design all the way through to supervising its assembly on the exhibition floor.

Design houses may offer similar benefits; but with numerous departments and employees, ranging from estimators through to project controllers, should also be in a position to provide extensive, hands-on expertise in all areas. Obviously, their charges are significantly higher and they tend to be cost-effective only for more substantial projects, such as a free-build stand at larger trade and popular consumer shows. It is likely that they will not be suitable for you on this occasion.

Many contractors offer stand design services for a limited or even no fee (although a 'free' service is invariably built into the overall construction package price). Obviously, it can appear to be inexpensive and convenient to employ the same organization to design and build your stand, especially if it is the on-site contractor nominated by the organizer. Nevertheless, there are drawbacks. A standardized design using at-hand materials may be produced, more suited to the contractor's requirements than your own. By commissioning a contractor, you may be tied to using their construction services too, which you may not necessarily want to do. Also, it is not unknown for contractors to subcontract design services to a freelance designer or design house, so you will effectively be paying over the odds in some instances.

Before approaching anyone – possibly a freelance designer – you must decide what qualities ought to be possessed by this particular specialist. He or she should be sufficiently talented and imaginative enough to design a stand that conveys the right image, is attractive and provides a quality working environment, all in a fresh and original fashion. You do not want a rehash of 1,001 other stands. The designer must be fully experienced in exhibition stand design rather than in related (but quite different) design fields so that he or she knows what works and does not work at a show. Ideally, he or she should also have some specific experience of your type of firm, products, services, customers, rivals, marketplace, exhibition and stand, as preparing a design for a nuts and bolts wholesaler at a local show is different from one for a house builder at an international event. The more hands-on experience that he or she has in your territory, the better the results will probably be.

You will further wish to see that the designer is reputable and will disclose rival commissions to you and shall maintain confidentiality at all times: you do not want details of your revolutionary new product to be leaked before it is unveiled on the opening day of the event. Similarly, you wish to be sure that you are receiving independent and impartial advice which is right for you, and is not being given because the designer wants to palm you off with rejected ideas from another commission or materials left over from the previous job. Compatibility is important too. As in any professional relationship, it is necessary for you, your team, the designer and his or her team to work together well, with everyone pulling in the same direction.

Financial stability has to be taken into account, especially when operating in difficult trading conditions. Clearly, you do not want to commission a designer only to find that the business subsequently runs into financial problems or even ceases trading during the run-up to the exhibition. As a consequence, your plans could be ruined. Likewise, you need to be certain that you will receive value-for-money services, and will not be exploited because of your inexperience in the field. Typically, fees are set by an hourly rate or as a percentage of the total, estimated production costs and should be agreed upon commission. Often, they become payable in stages, perhaps on commission, after the design is accepted and at the end of the show. Expenses – for telephone calls, travel and so on – are usually added to the final bill as well.

Knowing what you want, you then need to draw up a list of perhaps three to six designers whom you can approach to discuss your requirements before formally providing your choice with a brief and commissioning him or her to work on your behalf. You can prepare such a shortlist by contacting the trade body known as The Chartered Society of Designers which maintains a register containing detailed information about its members and their areas of expertise; see Appendix D: 'Useful contacts', page 135. These designers abide by the Society's code of conduct, which is good news for their clients. Alternatively, or better still as well, approach the exhibition organizer, trade associations such as the Agricultural Show Exhibitors Association, British Exhibition Contractors Association and the National Exhibitors Association plus personal contacts for recommendations. Refer to Chapter 2: 'Who's who at exhibitions', page 6, and Appendix D: 'Useful contacts', page 135.

Whether meeting shortlisted designers on your or their premises (or preferably both on successive occasions), you need to tell them all about yourself. Talk of and show them around the firm, encouraging them to sit in on discussions, perhaps concerning budgets, marketing and advertising strategies and goals. Introduce them to key colleagues, outlining roles and responsibilities. Let them see products used and services performed, examining and testing goods, as appropriate. Chat about customers and competitors too, possibly giving them the opportunity to meet and talk to some of the customers, if relevant. Discuss the show, the venue, the organizer and the anticipated exhibitors and visitors, sharing the information which you have with them so that they develop as detailed an understanding of everything as you possess.

Question the designers about themselves to see how they match the qualities required. As and when appropriate, you might raise such queries as: Do you belong to your trade organization? When did you begin trading? How is your business organized? Who are the owners and key employees? What are their backgrounds? What qualifications do they possess? What are their areas of expertise? Who else have you worked for? What other commissions do you have at the moment? Do you act on behalf of any of my rivals? These and other questions which arise during the course of your conversations should enable you to go some way towards deciding whether the designers are experienced, reputable and so forth.

Further thought can be directed towards how far the designers match your various requirements by visiting them at their offices, to assess the working environment, their staff and so on. Seeing them on their home ground may enable you to ascertain whether they are busy and professional in their approach, and if the atmosphere towards you is warm or frosty. You can watch them in action, checking their work and discussing their backgrounds, experiences and expertise with them in some depth. Hopefully, firm conclusions can be reached about their talents, imagination and all-round suitability for you.

You then need to work through your workload and what you want a designer to do on your behalf. Obviously, you will talk about the proposed type, size and site of your stand, with your ideas for its appearance, contents and working areas. Perhaps you wish the designer to produce a scale drawing and explanation of the stand as well as a scale model for clarification, and to avoid confusion and misunderstandings later on. Typically, you will also wish him or her to forward the agreed design to the organizer for permission, attend to any necessary amendments, employ a contractor and supervise the construction of the stand for you. In return, the designers will talk to you about work schedules and likely fees and expenses.

With a clear idea in your mind of who you want to commission, you should ask for the names and telephone numbers of their past and present clients so that you can contact these people for reference purposes. Telephone rather than write to them for off-the-record comments. Raise questions such as: How pleased were you with their work? Was it fresh and original? Was it well suited to your individual needs? Did they act in a professional and efficient manner? If not, what happened? Did you like and trust them, and their advice? Did they complete their work on time? Was it in budget? Did their work represent value for money? Would you use them again? If not, why not?

Hopefully, you can then make your choice, forwarding your detailed brief to the favoured designer. It is always wise at this stage to have everything agreed and noted down in writing, referring any written agreement to a solicitor if necessary. Whether in a letter or a formal contract, you and the designer should set out the precise brief, workload and schedule, fees, likely expenses and payment arrangements, before signing the document. Other designers who were under consideration ought to be thanked and rejected politely.

## Employing a contractor

It is likely that your selected designer will take charge of employing a contractor to build your stand under his or her instruction and supervision. Nevertheless, you should be broadly aware of what the process ought to involve, if tackled properly. As with choosing a designer, it is wise to initially identify the qualities which should exist in the winning contractor. You might want to pick one who is sufficiently talented, fully experienced in stand design, specifically experienced in your field, reputable, compatible, financially stable and cost-effective, all for much the same reasons.

Again, a shortlist of contractors should be compiled. Contact the British Exhibition Contractors Association which can supply details of its members who must abide by its code of conduct and recommended conditions of contract. See pages 87 to 89. This is reassuring news for you. In addition, talk to the exhibition organizer and other trade associations such as the Agricultural Show Exhibitors Association and the National Exhibitors Association.

See Chapter 2: 'Who's who at exhibitions', page 6 and Appendix D: 'Useful contacts', page 135.

It is then usual for you – or more probably your designer – to approach the listed contractors, submitting documents and asking them to tender for the contract. Depending upon the complexity of the task – varying from adding display panels to a shell scheme to constructing a complex, free-build stand – you would provide working drawings to illustrate the work, specifications to describe it and a set of the exhibition organizer's rules and regulations (see pages 69 to 74). On receipt of tenders, you may wish to arrange meetings to discuss your requirements along similar lines as before, prior to taking up references, making your choice and rejecting the other contractors.

In many cases, exhibitors and contractors operate with gentlemen's agreements based upon correspondence, discussions and handshakes. Clearly, this is naive as it creates opportunities for confusion at best, and exploitation at worst. It is advisable to have everything written down and signed by both parties before work commences. Typically, acceptance of a contractor's quote binds you to any terms and conditions that are printed on the reverse side, unless otherwise agreed in writing. Hence, this small print should be viewed as a starting point, to be read by you and a solicitor, with alterations, deletions and additions to develop from it. Hopefully, your contractor belongs to the British Exhibition Contractors Association and adheres to those fair and reasonable recommended conditions of contract. Even so, these conditions should be the beginning, not the end of the matter.

Make sure that roles and responsibilities are well defined, so both sides know who has to do what. Often, certain tasks are subcontracted by the contractor to outside specialists. Be certain the contractor remains responsible to you for *all* of the work carried out, including (and perhaps especially) those duties allocated to others. Ensure that the lines of communication are clear. For example, instructions and confirmations must pass through the designer, and changes and amendments should be put in writing. Have everything timetabled, so both parties know what has to be done, and by when. Be particularly careful to set a completion date. Make sure ownership of goods and materials is understood, and everyone is aware of what happens to them after the show. You do not want your reusable items to be junked. Be clear about fees, and payment arrangements too.

GENERAL CONDITIONS

1 INTERPRETATION

1.1 In these Conditions

'The Contractor' means the Member of the British Exhibition Contractors Association which agrees to perform the Contract Work.

'Contract Work' means any or all of the work which the Contractor agrees to perform and/or the services which the Contractor agrees to provide including the provision of Goods on hire or by sale.

'Goods' means all goods of whatsoever description including but not limited to materials, plant, equipment. machinery and fittings.

'Customer' means the person, firm or corporate body who agrees to purchase Contract Work.

'Contract' means any contract between the Contractor and the Customer for the carrying out of Contract Work.

1.2 Any reference in these Conditions to any provision of a statute shall be construed as a reference to that provision as amended, re-enacted or extended at the relevant time.

1.3 The headings in these Conditions are for convenience only and shall not affect the interpretation of a Contract.

2 ORDERS AND SPECIFICATIONS

2.1 These Conditions shall apply to every Quotation and Contract. The Contractor shall not be bound by any terms or conditions which may be inconsistent with these Conditions.

2.2 No variation of, or addition to, these Conditions shall be effective unless in writing and signed by the Contractor.

2.3 Any advice or recommendation given by the Contractor or its employees or agents to the Customer concerning Contract Work prior to the making of the Contract to which it relates, which is not confirmed in writing by the Contractor when such Contract is made, is followed or acted upon entirely at the Customer's own risk and the Contractor shall not be liable for any such advice or recommendation.

2.4 Any typographical or clerical error or omission in any Quotation, price list, acceptance, invoice or other such document issued by the Contractor shall be subject to correction without any liability on the part of the Contractor.

2.5 All specifications, descriptions, drawings, designs, measures or other information provided by the Contractor in relation to Contract Work and/or Goods are approximate howsoever provided, shall not form part of a Contract and, with relation thereto, the Contractor reserves the right to incorporate modifications or amendments in Contract Work.

2.6 No Contract shall be created unless the Contractor has accepted in writing a Quotation acceptance or order placed by the Customer, irrespective of how such Quotation acceptance or order is expressed and whether it results from a prior quotation or arises otherwise.

2.7 The Customer shall be responsible to the Contractor for ensuring the accuracy of the terms of any order or other material (including any applicable specification) submitted by it or on its behalf and for giving the Contractor any necessary information relating to Contract Work within a sufficient time to enable the Contractor to perform the Contract in respect thereof in accordance with its terms.

2.8 The Customer shall be responsible to the Contractor for obtaining all necessary Licences and other permissions whatsoever for the performance of Contract Work.

2.9 The Customer shall be responsible for ensuring that every building, path, private road, open space or other property to be used in the performance of Contract Work is safe and suitable for the intended use and, without limitation of the foregoing, is adequately served with all required public utilities.

2.10 The Customer may not cancel a Contract unless the Contractor agrees in writing and then on the terms that the Customer shall indemnify the Contractor in full against all loss including loss of profit, costs (including the cost of all labour and materials used), claims, actions, damages, charges and expenses incurred by the Contractor as a result of cancellation.

2.11 The Contractor shall have and retain the property, copyright and all other intellectual or industrial property rights in drawings, designs, plans, models, specifications and/or estimates prepared by the Contractor.

2.12 Where the Customer is to supply goods ('Customer's Property') to the Contractor in connection with the Contract Work, risk in Customer's Property will remain in the Customer. The Contractor will not be liable to the Customer for loss of or any damage to Customer's Property unless caused by the negligent act or omission of the Contractor.

2.13 If any part of Contract Work is to be performed elsewhere than on the Contractor's premises, the Customer shall be responsible to the Contractor for insuring the place of performance of such Contract Work and shall indemnify the Contractor against liability for any damage to the place of performance of such Contract Work, however caused.

### 3 PRICES

3.1 The Contractor will quote for Contract Work only after the Contractor has received a written specification from, or on behalf of, the Customer.

3.2 The Contractor's Quotation shall be open for acceptance within either the period stated therein or, if none is stated, within three calendar months of its date.

3.3 The Contractor reserves the right by giving notice to the Customer at any time before completion of Contract Work to increase the price of the applicable Contract in the following circumstances:

3.3.1 Where additional work is performed at the Customer's request; and/or

3.3.2 to reflect any increase in the cost to the Contractor which is due to any factor beyond the Contractor's control (such as, without limitation, any foreign exchange fluctuation, currency regulation, alteration of duties, increase in the cost of labour, materials or other costs of performance) or any failure of the Customer to give the Contractor adequate information or instructions; and/or

3.3.3 without prejudice to the generality of condition 3.3.2 above, to reflect any increase in the general index of retail prices compiled by the United Kingdom Department of Employment and published in the United Kingdom in the monthly digest of statistics by the Central Statistical Office or any index substantially replacing it.

3.4 Prices are exclusive of VAT and, where applicable, any additional or substitute taxes, levies, imposts, duties, fees or charges whatsoever and wherever payable, all of which shall be paid by the Customer

### 4 TERMS OF PAYMENT

The Customer shall pay one half of the price of a Contract when it is made and shall pay the balance (including any extra sums due under Condition 3.3 above) on completion of Contract Work as notified by the Contractor or, where Contract Work relates to an exhibition, on the opening of the exhibition if earlier. Time for payment shall be of the essence. Receipts for payment will be issued only on request.

4.1 If the Customer fails to make any payment on the due date then, without prejudice to any other right or remedy available to the Contractor, the Contractor shall be entitled, at its option at any time thereafter to

4.1.1 terminate the relevant Contract and suspend further performance of Contract Work; and

4.1.2 require the immediate return of any Goods hired to the Customer and

4.1.3 full payment, without deduction, of the total amount due and/or which would have become due under the relevant Contract but for termination, together with interest (both before and after any judgement) on the amount overdue from time to time at the rate of 4% per annum above Midland Bank base rate from time to time until payment in full is made.

4.2 Property in Goods supplied by way of sale under a Contract shall not pass until payment by the Customer of all sums due under the Contract under which the Goods were delivered; until property in such Goods passes the Customer shall hold them as bailee for the Contractor, shall store them separately from all other property of the Customer or any third party, marked so as to be clearly identifiable as belonging to the Contractor, shall keep them insured against all usual risks in their full invoice value and if any of the events referred to in clause 9 occurs, the Customer shall place such Goods at the disposal of the Contractor and the Contractor shall be entitled to enter upon any premises of the Customer, or any other premises where such Goods are kept, for the purpose of removing them.

### 5 WARRANTY

Provided that notice is given as soon as reasonably possible, and in any event within seven days of the defect being discovered and Provided Always that in the case of goods such notice must be given within the period of hire, where supplied on hire, or within 12 months of the date of delivery where supplied by way of sale, if the Customer gives notice of a defect in Contract Work, and the Contractor is satisfied that a defect exists and was not caused in whole or in part by any matter, action or occurrence outside the Contractor's control the Contractor shall in its sole discretion either remedy the defect or refund to the Customer a reasonable proportion of the price of the Contract.

### 6 LIABILITY

6.1 The terms of Condition 5 are in lieu of all conditions warranties and statements of whatever nature in respect of Contract Work whether express or implied by statute, trade, custom or otherwise and any such condition, warranty or statement is hereby excluded.

6.2 The Contractor shall not be liable for any defect in Contract Work arising directly or indirectly from compliance with any drawing, design, specification or order of the Customer.

6.3 Without prqudice to the terms of Conditions 6.1 6.2 and 6.4 the Contractor will accept liability for any loss or damage sustained by the Customer as a direct result of any breach of a Contract or of any liability of the Contractor (including negligence) in respect of the performance of a Contract provided that such liability shall be limited to payment of damages not exceeding the invoice value of the Contract in question.

6.4 Subject to the terms of Condition 6.6, the Contractor shall not be liable for the following loss or damage howsoever caused (even if foreseeable or in the Contractor's contemplation):

6.4.1 Loss of profits, business or revenue whether sustained by the Customer or any other Person; and/or

6.4.2 special, indirect or consequential loss or damage, whether sustained by the Customer or any other person; and/or

6.4.3 any loss arising from any claim made against the Customer by any other Person.

6.5 The Customer shall indemnify the Contractor against all claims, actions, costs, expenses (including court costs and legal fees) or other liabilities whatsoever in respect of:

6.5.1 Any liability arising under the Consumer Protection Act 1967 unless caused by the negligent act or omission of the Contractor in the manufacture and/or supply of Goods; and/or

6.5.2 any claim for breach of industrial and/or intellectual property rights arising out of compliance with any drawings, designs, specifications or order of the Customer; and/or

6.5.3 any breach of Contract or negligent or wilful act or omission of the Customer in relation to a Contract.

6.6 These Conditions do not purport to exclude or restrict any liability the exclusion or restriction of which is prohibited by Sections 2(1) and 6(1) of the Unfair Contract Terms Act 1977.

NOTHING IN THESE CONDITIONS SHALL AFFECT THE STATUTORY RIGHTS OF A CONSUMER

## 7 HIRED GOODS

7.1 Unless specifically provided by way of sale, all Goods used or supplied by the Contractor in connection with Contract Work shall be deemed to be on hire to the Customer.

7.2 The Customer shall indemnify the Contractor against the loss of and/or damage to hired Goods howsoever caused.

7.3 The Customer shall keep hired Goods in his possession and/or under his control at all times and shall not remove them from the place where they are installed by the Contractor without the latter's prior written consent .

7.4 Upon expiry of the period of deemed hire, or upon the earlier termination of the relevant Contract, the Customer shall no longer be in possession of hired Goods and the Contractor may at any time without notice, retake possession of such hired Goods and the Contractor shall be entitled to enter the premises of the Customer and/or any other place of performance of Contract Work, for such purposes.

## 8 FORCE MAJEURE

The Contractor shall be entitled, without liability on its part and without prejudice to its other rights to terminate a Contract or any unfulfilled part thereof or at its option, to suspend or give partial performance under it, if performance by the Contractor or by its suppliers is prevented, hindered, or delayed whether directly or indirectly by reason of any cause whatever beyond the Contractor's or its suppliers' reasonable control, whether such cause existed on the date when the Contract was made or not .

## 9 INSOLVENCY

If the Customer, being an individual, or being a firm, if any partner in the Customer is the subject of a petition for a bankruptcy order or of an application for an interim order under Part VIII of the Insolvency Act 1986, or if the Customer, being a company, compounds with its creditors or has a receiver or manager appointed in respect of all or any part of its assets or is the subject of an application for an administration order or of any proposal for a voluntary arrangement under Part I of the Insolvency Act 1986; or enters into liquidation whether compulsorily or voluntarily otherwise than for the purpose of amalgamation or reconstruction, or if the Contractor reasonably believes that any of the above events is about to occur, then the Contractor shall be entitled immediately, and at any time thereafter, to terminate forthwith any Contract or any unfulfilled part thereof.

## 10 GENERAL

10.1 No waiver by the Contractor of any breach of Contract by the Customer shall be construed as a waiver of any subsequent breach of the same or any other provision.

10.2 If any provision of these Conditions is held by any competent authority to be invalid or unenforceable in whole or in part the validity of the other provisions of these Conditions and the remainder of the provision in question shall not be affected thereby.

10.3 Any dispute arising under or in connection with these Conditions or the work done by the Contractor shall be referred to arbitration by a single arbitrator appointed by agreement or (in default) nominated on the application of either party.

10.4 This Contract shall be governed by the Laws of England.

## Summary

1. Potential exhibitors should not produce DIY stands as this is a specialized and highly skilled activity. Ideally, would-be exhibitors will simply possess numerous ideas and then:
   - commission a designer to turn them into reality
   - employ a contractor to physically create them.

2. Design services can be obtained from several sources, most notably:
   - freelance designers
   - design houses
   - contractors.

3. All designers should possess certain key qualities. They must be:
   - talented and imaginative
   - experienced in exhibition stand design
   - knowledgeable, if possible, in the exhibitor's area of activity
   - reputable
   - compatible
   - financially stable
   - able to offer a 'value-for-money' service.

4. A designer can be chosen by:
   - shortlisting three to six after contacting and talking to the appropriate trade body
   - discussing the exhibitor's background with the shortlisted designers
   - questioning them about their work
   - detailing requirements as precisely as possible
   - taking up references
   - making the choice.

5. Normally, the selected designer will instruct a contractor to actually build the stand. When approaching this task, the designer may:
   - identify the qualities required of the chosen contractor – talent, experience, and so on
   - speak to the relevant trade association, and other advisers, to produce a shortlist
   - put the contract out to tender
   - discuss the requirements with the parties involved and take up references
   - reach a decision.

6. Once the contractor has been employed, it is important that the relationship between the exhibitor and that contractor is:
   - specified in writing
   - agreed clearly in advance by both parties
   - well defined
   - clear and open.

# 9 Having a successful exhibition

IF YOU HAVE APPROACHED EXHIBITING at a consumer, trade or private show in a careful and thorough manner, you should now be well prepared and able enough to go on and become a successful exhibitor at your first event. Working in close collaboration with your designer and/or your contractor, you must set about maintaining your schedule, running the stand and evaluating results which will hopefully all combine to bring your activities to a winning conclusion.

## Maintaining your schedule

Having previously sketched out a list of activities that needed to be attended to up and beyond the exhibition and with some of these tasks already completed, you must now consider the remaining activities again. Having regrouped the various tasks from beneath the headings of the stand, exhibits, staff, promotional and other activities into a new order based on deadlines, you should set about tackling them properly and on time. See Chapter 6: 'Choosing exhibitions', page 47.

Clearly, several tasks will be handed over to your designer and/or contractor. These might include filling in forms in good time to obtain workers' passes from the exhibition organizer, hiring or buying display items on your behalf and arranging for exhibits and display materials to be lifted into place, assembled and installed under supervision. Also, they should book electricity, gas and other services from the organizer, supervise the erection of the stand and ensure that all of the services required are provided as agreed.

Other tasks will be dealt with by you. A significant proportion of them are relatively mundane and can be carried out smoothly, assuming that they are approached early and in a co-ordinated fashion. You may have to reserve accommodation for yourself and your staff in a comfortable and conveniently sited hotel. Do this as soon as possible, as the most popular hotels and rooms can fill up quickly once the previous event has ended. It may be necessary to complete forms in plenty of time to receive badges, exhibitor's passes, invitations to entertainments such as a dinner dance and car parking tickets from the organizer.

Make sure that you ask for sufficient numbers of them to avoid petty wranglings and squabbles later on.

Substantial stocks of technical and sales literature should be kept on the stand for staff to refer to and hand out to customers. Submit orders for these well in advance. Similarly, ensure stationery is readily available, including notepads, enquiry forms, business cards, order books and sales invoices. Exhibits and other display items must be made, examined and be ready for transporting to the contractor or (more likely) the exhibition on the agreed dates. You will need to make or confirm travel arrangements for yourself and your staff, deciding whether to use individual cars or to hire a minibus for everyone.

Often overlooked – and bitterly regretted afterwards – is the insurance of your staff, exhibits, display items and stand when in transit and at the event. Also protect yourself against the possibility that the show may be postponed or cancelled, with the potential loss of significant expenditure. Arrange temporary cover by adapting your existing policy through your insurance broker or company. Check beforehand though to see what insurance has been taken out by your designer, contractor, organizer and venue owner to make certain that you do not duplicate cover, adding unnecessarily to your expenses.

Some activities which you must tackle are less routine and require careful thought and consideration. You have to appoint a stand manager to administer and run the stand. In all probability, you will take this supervisory role. If not, whoever is chosen must be as familiar with your firm, products and services, goals and so on as you now are. You also need to select the right numbers of stand staff. Too many, and they may crowd out visitors and have little to do. Too few, and they could be overrun and miss out on sales leads.

Contemplate the type of stand staff required. Pick sales employees who know the goods inside out, are familiar with selling techniques and who are able to talk to people from the most junior to senior visitor. Balance out the numbers with technicians who can deal with technical queries, public relations employees tc handle customer complaints and media enquiries, and other staff as appropriate, such as cleaners, caterers and interpreters at an international event. It is wise to seek a blend of individual specialists working together in harmony rather than non-specialist staff who have to do everything and usually do so with mixed results. Decide whether to dress staff in uniforms which can help them to stand out from the crowd and convey a co-ordinated image of your firm.

A staff rota has to be drawn up well before the event, indicating who is on the stand and when. Employees need to be at their best to do their job properly and being on show for lengthy periods can be extremely stressful and tiring, so it is sensible to allow a thirty-minute break after being on duty for three hours or more. Also, be careful to ensure that both the numbers and types of staff on the stand remain above or at certain minimum levels at all times, as leaving the stand undermanned or without key specialists especially at busy periods can be harmful to the business, in terms of weakened image and missed sales opportunities.

Your staff ought to be briefed prior to the exhibition. Fill in all the background details about the firm, products and services, goals, customers, rivals, market and budget, as relevant to them. Invite questions and provide answers about appropriate topics such as production schedules, delivery times, how the show fits in to your overall objectives and so on. Then talk about: the venue and its location, layout and facilities; the organizer and their plans; the show with dates and opening times; the stand, outlining its type, size, site, the exhibits, display materials and so forth; the other exhibitors, particularly your rivals; miscellaneous, personal information, such as hotel and travel arrangements, uniforms, rotas, stand do's and don't's and so on. Provide written notes of the main points in a folder, for subsequent reference and use.

You may wish to offer additional training too. This could simply involve reading relevant books or watching videos on exhibiting and related topics such as handling customers on a face-to-face basis; see Appendix E: 'Recommended reading', page 137. Alternatively, you might arrange for them (and indeed you) to attend training courses such as those linked with the National Exhibitors Association and the Incorporated Society of British Advertisers Limited. Do so in good time. Refer to Chapter 2: 'Who's who at exhibitions', page 6 and Appendix D: 'Useful contacts', page 135.

Promotional and advertising activities must be carried out as well. You should compile a prospects list of key, existing and would-be customers, arranging for direct mail shots to be sent to them publicizing your presence at the show and inviting them along. Enclose complimentary tickets to the show and associated entertainments, if appropriate. Send press releases to the media, especially any contacts that you have in the local, regional or trade press who might give you a good write-up. Sales agents should be instructed to spread the news of your imminent attendance at the exhibition, and what may happen there.

Also, you must submit your free entry to the show catalogue by the deadline set by the organizer, otherwise your details will be added to the addendum sheets which are usually lost or thrown away. Use all of your allocated number of words, outlining your firm, products and services, telephone and fax numbers and a contact name, perhaps your own. Typically, these catalogues are only glanced at during the exhibition to help visitors find the exhibitors they want to see. However, they are usually then kept as a reference guide, being dipped into on and off until the next event is staged. Hence, concentrate on conveying an image of your business and what it does, rather than on what you are exhibiting at this show.

Compile press kits – perhaps comprising press releases about your firm, goods, services and goals plus photographs of your stand, staff and exhibits – for distribution to the media as and when required. Give them what they want to know, making it easy for them to write favourable previews and reviews about you. Do not overlook your other advertising activities in the press, radio and other media during the build up, possibly drawing in references to your attendance at the exhibition, and your plans thereafter.

Various other duties will need to be carried out after the show has ended and ought to be thought about and planned in anticipation. Your designer and/or contractor will normally have to make certain that the stand, exhibits and all other items are dismantled, removed and returned to the appropriate places within a day or so of the exhibition. You must ensure they have been clearly instructed to do this. Also, you should compile further press releases announcing the winning of an award, signature of a large contract or whatever. Contacts made at the show ought to be followed up with direct mail shots being sent out, telephone calls made and sales visits arranged. Staff should be debriefed, with a full review of the exhibition taking place; see Chapter 6: 'Choosing exhibitions', page 47.

## Running the stand

As stand manager, you, or a fully briefed colleague, should act in an administrative and advisory capacity. It is your overall role to make certain that staff follow the do's and don't's of stand success, to ensure the stand is maintained in a fit and proper manner and to attend to those after-show duties. It is important to restrict yourself to supervisory and co-ordinating responsibilities only, pulling everyone and everything together. Leave sales, technical and public relations duties to fellow, appropriately qualified personnel.

You need to draw your stand staff's attention to several do's, some of which are probably familiar or instinctive to sales people, but are less so to others. Do have plenty of sleep beforehand, to sustain you through a long and tiring day. Do wear the agreed clothes and badges as planned and at all times, to convey a unified, professional image of the firm. Familiarize yourself with the flow patterns on and around the stand, taking up strategic positions during quieter moments. Greet visitors with a smile and a nod, while allowing them time to breathe and establish their interest before approaching them.

Open by asking a question such as 'What do you like about . . . ?' or 'How does this compare to . . . ?', which should elicit a full response that can be developed into a conversation. Be polite and interested in the visitor and what he or she has to say. Look and sound enthusiastic about the business, products, show and so on. If you are not, you cannot expect the visitor to be either. Stick to what you know, passing the visitor over to a colleague if he or she is better informed on a particular (sales, technical or public relations) subject. Note the numbers and types of visitors, take business cards, record enquiries, write down orders, sales and so forth on a regular basis.

Remain alert to spot would-be vandals and thieves who appear at many exhibitions, especially if small goods, product samples, alcohol and food are on the stand. Lock away valuables, taking them out and returning them to storage as and when required. Notify security staff whenever assistance is needed. Take regular breaks to refresh yourself. Be careful about what you eat and drink during these times. Try to take a walk outside the venue to clear your mind, ease the pressure and recharge your batteries. You, and your staff, can probably think of other do's to share with each other.

Of course, there are various don't's that have to be pointed out to stand personnel, time and again if necessary. Don't overeat or drink too much the night before if you want to survive the next day. Don't wear tight clothes or new shoes which will make you feel extremely uncomfortable as time passes. Never eat, smoke, drink, swear, read books or newspapers within sight or sound of a visitor, all of which will harm your polished, quality image. Wait until your next break to do any of these. Only sit down if it is to talk to a visitor. Avoid looking bored or redundant. Busy yourself instead by tidying up the surroundings.

Do not stand around in groups; this is offputting to visitors. Similarly, avoid 'Roll up! Roll up!' stances or guard-like positions which are both unappealing. Never block entrances or obscure exhibits or display materials: visitors have not come to see what you look like. Be careful not to work in pairs, which can appear threatening and may alienate visitors. Try not to hover, trail or chase a visitor across the stand – you will simply drive him or her away. When starting a would-be discussion, don't say 'Can I help you?' 'No' ends the conversation before it even began.

During a talk, steer clear of patronizing the visitor, either by using technical jargon or over-simplified phrases. Find out who the person is and adjust your language accordingly. Don't tell him or her about what interests you. Discover what he or she wants to know and pass on the information in a clear and concise manner. Never become flustered if you cannot answer a question yourself. Be ready to refer to a colleague, technical or promotional literature when appropriate. End on a positive note, by handing out a catalogue and price list or exchanging business cards which can be followed up. You, and other stand personnel, may be able to list more don't's to be discussed between you.

The stand itself must be maintained in good order for the duration of the show if it is to continue to put across the right image, attract visitors to it and provide a first-rate working environment for everyone at all times. The organizer will typically be in charge of keeping the surrounding areas clean and tidy while you take responsibility for your own individual stand, although you may have arranged for stand cleaning to be provided before or after the day's activities; this is very sensible.

Whatever the cleaning arrangements, a busy stand will soon acquire a grubby, well-worn appearance unless everyone involved makes a positive and ongoing effort to keep it looking neat and tidy throughout the day. You and your staff should: hang up coats out of sight; put briefcases, bags and other personal possessions away in cupboards; remove dirty cups from view; pick up rubbish; straighten stationery and literature, disposing of dog-eared and scribbled-on copies; top up stationery and literature supplies as necessary; check for damage to the stand, exhibits and display items, contacting the on-site contractor or replacing as appropriate; keep entrances, chairs, floors and exits free from obstructive articles.

Do remember the after-show activities that you are responsible for. Tell newspapers, magazines and other media about any good news which happened at or was generated by the exhibition. Publicize the 'Product of the Year' award, the huge export order from overseas and so on. If you do not promote yourself, you cannot expect anyone else to do it on your behalf. Follow through on all leads. Study notes made, enquiry forms completed and business cards taken to decide which contacts should be telephoned, written to or visited by a sales agent. The show does not – or at least should not – end on the final day. The successful exhibitor chases up visitors, turning casual and definite interests alike into hard sales.

Staff should be debriefed after the exhibition while it is still fresh in their minds. Try to ensure that everyone attends – you, sales, technical, public relations and other staff plus the designer and/or contractor if possible. In much the same way that you previewed the venue, organizer, show, exhibitors, visitors, stand and so on, you now need to review them in the light of your actual participation. Ask and listen to what everyone has to say about these many and varied aspects. See Chapter 6: 'Choosing exhibitions', page 47.

## Evaluating results

Naturally, you ought to measure and evaluate the results of exhibiting at your first show to see how far it has helped you towards achieving your goals. It is wise to refresh your memory if necessary and set out again exactly what your objectives were. You may have wanted to achieve a certain volume and/or value of sales, could have sought information about a new marketplace or might have wished to have changed or improved the image of your firm. In all probability, you had a mix of different goals. Refer to Chapter 3: 'Thinking about yourself', page 27.

It is relatively easy to measure how far you have moved towards achieving your financial objectives through your exhibiting activities if you and your staff faithfully recorded the numbers and types of visitors to your stand, enquiries and the volume and values of orders taken and sales made. You can simply add up visitors, enquiries, orders and sales and subsequently compare them alongside your targets. You may then decide for yourself how successful it was and whether your attendance was worthwhile.

You can place your findings into a more significant context by judging visitors, enquiries, orders and sales in relation to the cost of exhibiting. You should now be in a position to ascertain the actual rather than the estimated expenses involved with your stand, exhibits, promotional and other activities and be able to total up the final bill; see Chapter 5: 'Setting a budget', page 41. From here it is simple to calculate the cost per visitor, enquiry, order and sale of attending the show. If you keep similar records for sending out mail shots, advertising in the press and radio, having sales agents on the road and so forth, you can draw more conclusions about the viability of exhibitions as a sales medium.

Clearly, any assumptions that are made must take full account of the particular circumstances of this first show. For example, as a new exhibitor, it would be surprising if mistakes were not made and opportunities missed, whereas you may be more experienced in using other media. Also, numerous influences – bad weather, a transport strike, even a bomb scare – could have had knock-on effects. Consider the specific characteristics of exhibitions too. As an example, many visitors come to look and learn, and sales may follow on weeks or even months later; credit needs to be given to the show, when these eventually arrive.

Of course, other results are less easy to measure and put into context. It is difficult to judge how much data you have learned about a market or how far your image has changed in the minds of your customers. It is equally hard to value the other benefits to be derived from exhibiting, especially those that are less prominent in other media: the establishment of a warm rapport with an existing or new customer, the receipt of a snippet of information about a niche that can be exploited and so on. You need to take account of these too.

Much of this evaluation process into your objectives can be conducted by you, working in association with your stand staff, designer and/or contractor. Additional useful details during your assessments can sometimes be provided by the show organizer who may commission a general exhibition survey, subsequently selling its findings to exhibitors. For an appropriate fee, you can have questions inserted into this survey. As an example, you might wish visitors to be asked about their knowledge and views of your goods before and after the event.

Alternatively, you could employ a specialist company such as Exhibition

# MEDIA ASSESSMENT FORM

Campaign:

Number:

| Medium | Cost incurred (£) | Number of enquiries | Cost per enquiry (£) | Number of orders | Cost per order (£) | Total sales | Average sale per enquiry (£) | Average sale per order (£) | Comment |
|--------|-------------------|---------------------|----------------------|------------------|--------------------|-------------|------------------------------|----------------------------|---------|
| | | | | | | | | | |

Medium:

Date:

Completed by:                    Signature:                    Checked by:                    Signature:

**Media assessment form**

Surveys Limited to act on your behalf. Using a mix of face-to-face interviews, telephone conversations and postal questionnaires they can find out abut visitors' interests, reactions to and opinions of the show, their recall of exhibitors, memories of the stands etc. If you are unable to evaluate key goals by yourself, consider employing an independent expert to assist you. The expense involved is a small price to pay to establish the success or failure of your exhibition activities. Refer to Chapter 2: 'Who's who at exhibitions', page 6, Chapter 8: 'Using specialists', page 82 and Appendix D: 'Useful contacts', page 135. The 'Media assessment' form on page 98 may help you to evaluate your results.

## Summary

1. Those prospective exhibitors who have planned thoroughly are most likely to have a successful exhibition. To ensure this, they need to:
   - maintain their schedule
   - run the stand effectively
   - evaluate the results of their first exhibition.

2. Maintaining a schedule often involves:
   - making a note of the remaining activities that need to be carried out
   - putting them into a new order according to their deadlines
   - sharing them out, with some being passed to the designer and/or contractor.

3. The majority of activities will need to be retained and dealt with by the exhibitor. These include:
   - mundane tasks, such as form filling, ordering and insurance matters
   - more complex issues, like staff selection, organization and training
   - promotional work, such as advertising and composing press kits
   - miscellaneous duties like clearing up after the event.

4. To run a stand effectively, everyone working on it should:
   - understand and follow the do's and don'ts of stand management
   - keep it in good order, and clean and tidy too
   - attend promptly to after-show activities
   - attend a debriefing session after the event.

5. Each and every exhibition should be evaluated, with the results being compared and contrasted with:
- the initial objectives set
- the estimated costs of exhibiting
- the overall circumstances on this occasion.

# Conclusion: the exhibitor's checklist

HOPEFULLY, YOU WILL CONSIDER your attendance at your first show to be a resounding success and will wish to exhibit again. Prior to doing this though, you should review your activities to date to spot where achievements might be built upon and improvements could be made. Looking at and learning from the past increases your chances of a more successful future. Taking each stage in turn, ask yourself these questions to see whether you can respond in a positive manner to all of them. If not, make sure that you will be able to next time.

## Types of exhibition

❑ Were you fully aware of the characteristics of consumer, trade and private exhibitions?

❑ Did you recognize the potential benefits of exhibiting at a show, whether a consumer, trade or private event?

❑ Were you conscious of the possible drawbacks of attending a consumer, trade or private exhibition?

❑ Did you compare and contrast these various characteristics, pluses and minuses in relation to your own firm and circumstances?

## Who's who at exhibitions

❑ Did you know about the key participants at a show, and how they all work together?

❑ Were you familiar with the representative bodies in the exhibition industry, and what they can do to help you?

❏ Were you up to date with the other organizations associated with the industry, and how they might assist you?

❏ Did you contact anyone and everyone for advice and guidance?

## Thinking about yourself

❏ Did you possess a complete understanding of your own concern, and its distinctive mix of positive and negative features?

❏ Were you wholly conversant with your goods and services, and their specific strengths and weaknesses?

❏ Were you in touch with your short-, medium- and long-term, business goals?

❏ Did you compose notes about your firm, products, services and objectives for later reference?

## Recognizing your market

❏ Did you discover as much as you could about your customers and their characteristics, habits and opinions?

❏ Were you aware of your competitors and their goods, services and exhibition activities?

❏ Did you understand your market, and any changes and developments that were occurring within it?

❏ Did you conduct additional research as and where required, to fill in any gaps in your knowledge of the marketplace?

❏ Did you compile notes about your customers, rivals and market for subsequent use?

## Setting a budget

❏ Did you appreciate all of the possible costs that could be incurred when exhibiting at an event?

❑   Did you know which expenses were most relevant to you in your given situation?

❑   Were you conscious of the total expenditure involved in attending a show?

## Choosing exhibitions

❑   Did you prepare a shortlist of potentially suitable exhibitions by studying a lengthy list of shows alongside your extensive background notes?

❑   Did you obtain as much detailed material as you could from the organizers of the various events?

❑   Did you analyse all aspects of each exhibition, seeking advice from many sources before making your choice?

❑   Were you familiar with the different types of stand, and how to select the right size and site for your business?

❑   Did you check the organizer's rules and regulations with the help of a solicitor, prior to booking space?

❑   Did you draft a timetable of activities leading up to and beyond the show so you knew what to do and when?

## Designing a stand

❑   Were you aware of the key functions of an exhibition stand, and how these might be best achieved?

❑   Did you select exhibits and display items which were appropriate for the occasion?

❑   Did you sketch out a full and detailed brief for the person responsible for designing your stand?

❑   Were you wise enough to avoid adopting a DIY approach to designing the exhibition stand?

## Using specialists

❑ Did you consider the different types of designer who exist, and the key qualities that they ought to possess?

❑ Did you investigate your possible choices carefully, to see that they had all of the required qualities?

❑ Was everything agreed in writing before commissioning your designer?

❑ Did you contemplate your chosen contractor in the same way, and in as much depth?

❑ Did you obtain external advice and assistance before employing your contractor?

❑ Did you study any contract with your solicitor, before signing it?

## Having a successful exhibition

❑ Did you keep to your schedule, completing all of the tasks on or before the set deadlines?

❑ Did you and your staff follow the do's and don't's of stand success?

❑ Was your stand maintained in a fit and proper manner?

❑ Did you attend to the after-show activities, adopting a swift and effective approach?

❑ Did you evaluate how far your goals were achieved, seeking outside help and guidance as necessary?

# Appendix A: Exhibitions, 1997

For easy reference, exhibitions scheduled for 1997 are categorized under the following headings:

Architecture/Building
Automotive/Motoring
Business/Management
Catering/Food
Commerce/Industry
Computers/Business equipment
Construction/Public works
Decorating/Interiors/Design
Electrical/Lighting
Electronics/Telecommunications
Energy/Power/Environment/Water
Engineering/Machinery
Farming/Agriculture
Finance/Insurance/Banking/Law
Freighting/Transport
Government/Defence/Education
Hardware/Do it yourself

Health/Medicine
Marine/Aviation
Materials/Packaging/Processing
Mining/Metals
Petroleum/Chemicals
Printing/Photography/Books
Property/Real estate
Purchasing/Retailing
Radio/Television/Video
Recreation/Sports/Hobbies
Safety/Security
Science/Technology
Textiles/Clothing
Travel/Timesharing
Wildlife/Pets
Wines/Spirits/Brewing
Women/Home/Gardening

## Architecture/Building

Feb 16–18   **Pooltrade 97 – Swimming Pool News Trade Exhibition**
            *Venue:* Metropole Exhibition Centre, Brighton. *Organizer:* S.P.N. Exhibitions.
            01483 306304
Mar 11–13   **Maintec 97 – 20th National Maintenance Management Show**
            *Venue:* NEC, Birmingham. *Organizer:* Conference Communication. 01252
            783111
Mar 20–23   **Individual Homes – Home Building & Renovation Show**
            *Venue:* NEC, Birmingham. *Organizer:* Centaur Exhibitions. 0171 287 5678
Apr DTBA    **Architecture & Construction Show**
            *Venue:* Gleneagles. *Organizer:* Trade Exhibitions Scotland. 01786 880255
Nov 23–28   **Interbuild 97**
            *Venue:* NEC, Birmingham. *Organizer:* Andry Montgomery Ltd. 0171 486 1951
Nov 23–28   **Restorex/Refurbex 97 – 6th Products & Services for Building Restoration &
            Refurbishment Exhibition**
            *Venue:* NEC, Birmingham. *Organizer:* Mack-Brooks Exhibitions Ltd. 01707
            275641

**Automotive/Motoring**

Jan 7–10 **Autosport International**
*Venue:* NEC, Birmingham. *Organizer:* Haymarket Exhibitions Ltd. 0171 402 2555

Jan 25–26 **The Footman James Bristol Classic Motorcycle Show**
*Venue:* Exhibition Pavilions, Bristol. *Organizer:* Nationwide Exhibitions UK Ltd.
0117 970 1370

Feb 1–2 **The Footman James Bristol Classic Car Show**
*Venue:* Exhibition Pavilions, Bristol. *Organizer:* Nationwide Exhibitions UK Ltd.
0117 970 1370

Feb 25–27 **SMMT Commercial Vehicle & Bodywork Show**
*Venue:* NEC, Birmingham. *Organizer:* Society for Motor Manufacturers & Traders
Ltd. 0171 235 7000

Mar 15–16 **London Classic Motor Show**
*Venue:* Alexandra Palace, London. *Organizer:* Greenwoods Exhibitions. 01296
631181

Apr 19–20 **National Custom & Sports Car Show**
*Venue:* Exhibition Centre, Doncaster. *Organizer:* National Custom & Sports Car
Show. 01302 783584

Apr 27–30 **SMMT Automotive Trade Show**
*Venue:* NEC, Birmingham. *Organizer:* Society for Motor Manufacturers & Traders
Ltd. 0171 235 7000

Jun 1–2 **Forecourt Show, Forecourt Shop & Convenience Retailing Exhibition 97**
*Venue:* NEC, Birmingham. *Organizer:* Blenheim Group plc. 0181 742 2828

Oct 16–26 **The London Motor Show**
*Venue:* Earls Court, London. *Organizer:* P&O Events Limited. 0171 244 6433

Nov 4–6 **Autotech 97**
*Venue:* NEC, Birmingham. *Organizer:* IMechE – Institute of Mechanical Engineers.
0171 222 7899

Nov 13–23 **Scottish Motor Show**
*Venue:* SECC, Glasgow. *Organizer:* Scottish Motor Trade Association. 0131 225
3643

**Business/Management**

Jan 23–25 **Job Scene Merseyside**
*Venue:* St George's Hall, Liverpool. *Organizer:* T J W Exhibitions Ltd. 01823
433933

Jan 29–30 **Newcastle Business to Business Exhibition**
*Venue:* Racecourse, Newcastle. *Organizer:* Business Events Ltd. 0113 237 3022

Feb 4–5 **Intranet 97**
*Venue:* London. *Organizer:* Business Intelligence. 0181 544 1830

Feb 12–14 **Business Travel 97**
*Venue:* Business Design Centre, London. *Organizer:* Centaur Exhibitions. 0171 287
5678

Feb 18–20 **Spectra – Business to Business Exhibition**
*Venue:* SECC, Glasgow. *Organizer:* AR Trade Fairs Ltd. 01768 899739

Feb 21–22 **Job Scene South West**
*Venue:* The Pavilions, Plymouth. *Organizer:* T J W Exhibitions Ltd. 01823 433933

Feb 21–22 **North of England Franchise & Business Start Exhibition**
*Venue:* International Centre, Harrogate. *Organizer:* Positive Projects. 01846
603803

Mar 2–4 **Job Scene**
*Venue:* Docklands Arena, London. *Organizer:* T J W Exhibitions Ltd. 01823 433933

Mar 4–6      **HRD Week 97 – Human Resource Development Exhibition**
*Venue:* Wembley, London. *Organizer:* Touchstone Exhibitions & Conferences Ltd. 0181 332 0044

Mar 4–6      **Safety & Health at Work Exhibition 97**
*Venue:* Earls Court, London. *Organizer:* Paramount Exhibitions & Conferences. 0181207 5599

Mar 8–10      **FM Expo 97 – Facilities Management Conference & Exhibition**
*Venue:* Olympia, London. *Organizer:* Blenheim Group plc. 0181 742 2828

Mar 11–13      **Maintec 97 – 20th National Maintenance Management Show**
*Venue:* NEC, Birmingham. *Organizer:* Conference Communication. 01252 783111

Apr 15–17      **Offex – The Office Management Exhibition**
*Venue:* The Barbican Centre, London. *Organizer:* Showbusiness Exhibitions Ltd. 01992 788887

Apr 15–17      **The London Secretary Show**
*Venue:* The Barbican Centre, London. *Organizer:* Showbusiness Exhibitions Ltd. 01992 788887

Jun 18–19      **Business to Business Exhibition**
*Venue:* Hilton Hotel, Leeds. *Organizer:* Business Events Ltd. 0113 237 3022

Sep DTBA      **FM Expo North 97 – Facilities Management Conference & Exhibition**
*Venue:* G-Mex, Manchester. *Organizer:* Blenheim Group plc. 0181 742 2828

Oct DTBA      **The National Franchise Exhibition 97**
*Venue:* NEC, Birmingham. *Organizer:* Blenheim Group plc. 0181 742 2828

**Catering/Food**

Jan 20–23      **Hospitality Week**
*Venue:* NEC, Birmingham. *Organizer:* Reed Exhibition Company UK. 0181 910 7910

Feb 9–13      **IFE 97 – Int'l Food & Drink Exhibition**
*Venue:* Earls Court, London. *Organizer:* Andry Montgomery Ltd. 0171 486 1951

Mar 6–9      **BBC Good Food Show 97**
*Venue:* Olympia, London. *Organizer:* Consumer Exhibitions. 0181 948 1666

Mar 11–12      **Hotel & Catering Trade Exhibition**
*Venue:* International Centre, Bournemouth. *Organizer:* Bournemouth International Centre. 01202 552122

Mar 16–17      **Northern Catering & Food Fair 97**
*Venue:* Great Yorkshire Showground, Harrogate. *Organizer:* Southern Enterprise Exhibitions Ltd. 01252 734383

Mar 17–20      **Scothot 97 –13th Scottish Hotel, Catering & Licensed Trade Exhibition**
*Venue:* SECC, Glasgow. *Organizer:* Scottish Industrial & Trade Exhibitions Ltd. 0131 556 5152

Apr 8–9      **Welsh Catering & Food Fair 97**
*Venue:* Welsh Institute of Sport, Cardiff. *Organizer:* Southern Enterprise Exhibitions Ltd. 01252 734383

Apr 15–17      **NIFEX 97 – 6th Northern Ireland Int'l Food, Drink & Catering Exhibition**
*Venue:* Kings Hall, Belfast. *Organizer:* Industrial & Trade Exhibitions. 01232 230425

Apr 22–24      **Food & Drink Processing 97**
*Venue:* Olympia, London. *Organizer:* Reed Exhibition Company UK. 0181 910 7910

Sep 28–Oct 1      **Food & Bake 97**
*Venue:* NEC, Birmingham. *Organizer:* Turret Group plc. 01923 228577

**Commerce/Industry**

| | | |
|---|---|---|
| Jan 20–23 | **Hospitality Week 97** | |

*Venue:* NEC, Birmingham. *Organizer:* Reed Exhibition Company UK. 0181 910 7910

Jan 23–24 **Scottish Export Show**
*Venue:* Thistle Hotel. Glasgow. *Organizer:* Trade Exhibitions Scotland. 01786 880255

Mar 6–9 **The Great British Innovation & Inventions Fair**
*Venue:* Barbican Centre, London. *Organizer:* Sphinx Exhibitions Ltd. 01202 762252

Mar 19–20 **Midlands Manufacturing**
*Venue:* NEC, Birmingham. *Organizer:* European Trade & Exhibition Services Ltd. 01784 880890

Apr 29–May 1 **BCSSE 97 – The Cleaning Show**
*Venue:* NEC, Birmingham. *Organizer:* Turret Group plc. 01923 228577

Nov DTBA **Inspex – Quality Control & Inspection Technology Exhibition**
*Venue:* NEC, Birmingham. *Organizer:* Richmond Events Ltd. 0181 332 2422

Nov DTBA **Manufacturing Week 97**
*Venue:* NEC, Birmingham. *Organizer:* Reed Exhibition Company UK. 0181 910 7910

**Computers/Business Equipment**

Jan 8–11 **BETT 97 – Educational IT Exhibition**
*Venue:* Olympia, London. *Organizer:* EMAP Business Communications. 0171 388 2430

Feb 2–6 **Statindex – Office Products Exhibition**
*Venue:* NEC, Birmingham. *Organizer:* Trade Promotion Services Ltd. 0181 855 9201

Feb 4–5 **Intranet 97**
*Venue:* London. *Organizer:* Business Intelligence. 0181 544 1830

Mar 4–6 **ICAT 97 – Computer Integrated Technology for Design & Manufacturing Automation Event**
*Venue:* NEC, Birmingham. *Organizer:* EMAP Business Communications. 0171 388 2430

May 13–14 **Property Computer Show North**
*Venue:* Royal Armouries, Leeds. *Organizer:* VCM Communications. 01273 857800

May 22–25 **Comdef – Computer & Technology Reseller Forum**
*Venue:* Norwegian Crown Hotel, Dover. *Organizer:* Richmond Events Ltd. 0181 332 2422

Jun 10–11 **Headway Imaging IT – Document Imaging Exhibition**
*Venue:* Sandown Exhibition Centre, Esher. *Organizer:* Kingsgate Group, The. 01962 860670

Jun 24–26 **Data Base Expo 97**
*Venue:* NEC, Birmingham. *Organizer:* Blenheim Group plc. 0181 742 2828

Jun 24–26 **Networks 97**
*Venue:* NEC, Birmingham. *Organizer:* Blenheim Group plc. 0181 742 2828

Jun 24–26 **Software Development 97**
*Venue:* NEC, Birmingham. *Organizer:* Blenheim Group plc. 0181 742 2828

Jun 24–26 **Systems 97**
*Venue:* NEC, Birmingham. *Organizer:* Blenheim Group plc. 0181 742 2828

Sep 1–2      **Document – Business to Business Exhibition**
*Venue:* NEC, Birmingham. *Organizer:* Blenheim Group plc. 0181 742 2828

Sep DTBA    **ECTS – European Computer Trade Fair**
*Venue:* Olympia. London. *Organizer:* Blenheim Group plc. 0181 742 2828

Oct 1–2      **Scientific Computing Exhibition**
*Venue:* Sandown Exhibition Centre, Esher. *Organizer:* Institute of Physics. 0171 470 4800

Oct 7–9      **GIS 97 – Geographical Information Systems**
*Venue:* NEC, Bimmingham. *Organizer:* Blenheim Group plc. 0181 742 2828

Oct 21–22    **Property Computer Show**
*Venue:* New Connaught Rooms, London. *Organizer:* VCM Communications. 01273 857800

Nov 18–19    **Workplace 97 – Innovations in Office Furniture with Technology Exhibition**
*Venue:* Olympia, London. *Organizer:* Reed Exhibition Company UK. 0181 910 7910

## Construction/Public Works

Feb 18–20    **Construct IT**
*Venue:* Business Design Centre, London. *Organizer:* Framework Marketing & Sales. 01425 477565

Mar DTBA    **Huac – Highways Authorities & Utilities Committee 3rd National Conference & Exhibition**
*Venue:* ICC, Birmingham. *Organizer:* Westrade Group. 01923 778311

Apr DTBA    **Architecture & Construction Show**
*Venue:* Gleneagles. *Organizer:* Trade Exhibitions Scotland. 01786 880255

Apr 22–24    **Traffex 97 – Int'l Traffic Engineering & Road Safety Exhibition**
*Venue:* NEC, Birmingham. *Organizer:* Printerhall. 0171 436 7016

Nov 23–28    **Interbuild 97**
*Venue:* NEC, Birmingham. *Organizer:* Andry Montgomery Ltd. 0171 486 1951

## Decorating/Interiors/Design

Jan 16–Jul 19   **The Knitting Needlecraft and Design Exhibition**
*Venue:* Sandown Exhibition Centre, Esher. *Organizer:* Nationwide Exhibitions. 0117 970 1370

Jan 18–22    **Decorative Interiors 97**
*Venue:* NEC, Birmingham. *Organizer:* Blenheim Group plc. 0181 742 2828

Jan 19–22    **KBB 97 – Fitted Furniture, Decorative Interiors & Appliances Exhibition**
*Venue:* NEC, Birmingham. *Organizer:* Blenheim Group plc. 0181 742 2828

Jan 19–22    **The Furniture Show 97 – Incorporating Lighting & Furnishing Accessories**
*Venue:* NEC, Birmingham. *Organizer:* Blenheim Group plc. 0181 742 2828

Mar 13–Apr 6   **The Daily Mail Ideal Home Exhibition**
*Venue:* Earls Court, London. *Organizer:* DMG Trinity Ltd. 01895 677677

Mar 16–19    **Living Design London 97**
*Venue:* Battersea Park, London. *Organizer:* Ian Thompson Associates. 0171 833 3373

Apr 1–2      **Contract Interiors Exhibition**
*Venue:* Olympia, London. *Organizer:* Reed Exhibition Company UK. 0181 910 7910

Jun 11–15    **The London Furniture Show 97**
*Venue:* Earls Court, London. *Organizer:* London Furniture Show, The. 0181 941 8000

## Electrical/Lighting

Jan 19–22     **The Furniture Show 97 – Incorporating Lighting & Furnishing Accessories**
*Venue:* NEC, Birmingham. *Organizer:* Blenheim Group plc. 0181 742 2828

Jan 26–29     **Lightshow 97**
*Venue:* Earls Court, London. *Organizer:* Lighting Association, The. 01952 290905

## Electronics/Telecommunications

Mar 18–20     **Nepcon Electronics Exhibition**
*Venue:* NEC, Birmingham. *Organizer:* Reed Exhibition Company UK. 0181 910 7910

Mar 18–20     **Semiconductor Solutions Exhibition**
*Venue:* NEC, Birmingham. *Organizer:* Reed Exhibition Company UK. 0181 910 7910

Apr DTBA     **Infosec 97 – Information Security Exhibition**
*Venue:* Olympia, London. *Organizer:* Reed Exhibition Company UK. 0181 910 7910

May 22–25     **Comdef – Computer & Technology Reseller Forum**
*Venue:* Norwegian Crown Hotel, Dover. *Organizer:* Richmond Events Ltd. 0181 332 2422

Jun 24–26     **Networks 97**
*Venue:* NEC, Birmingham. *Organizer:* Blenheim Group plc. 0181 742 2828

Sep DTBA     **Live 97 – Consumer Electronics Show**
*Venue:* Earls Court, London. *Organizer:* Blenheim Group plc. 0181 742 2828

Oct DTBA     **Euro–EMC 97**
*Venue:* TBC. *Organizer:* Reed Exhibition Company UK. 0181 910 7910

## Energy/Power/Environment/Water

Mar 18–19     **Power Generation & Maintenance Exhibition**
*Venue:* Moat House Hotel, Glasgow. *Organizer:* FMJ International Publications Ltd. 01737 768611

Apr DTBA     **Energy Resource Exhibition**
*Venue:* NEC, Birmingham. *Organizer:* Reed Exhibition Company UK. 0181 910 7910

Apr 16–18     **ET 97 – Environmental Technology Exhibition**
*Venue:* NEC, Birmingham. *Organizer:* Reed Exhibition Company UK. 0181 910 7910

Jun 2–5     **Cired –14th Int'l Electricity Distribution Conference & Exhibition**
*Venue:* ICC, Birmingham. *Organizer:* IEE Conference Services. 0171 344 5478

Oct 7–9     **World Power & Energy Exhibition**
*Venue:* NEC, Birmingham. *Organizer:* Nexus Ltd. 01322 660070

Nov 4–6     **IWEX 97 – Int'l Water & Waste Industries Exhibition**
*Venue:* NEC, Birmingham. *Organizer:* Turret Group plc. 01923 228577

## Engineering/Machinery

Jan 21–23     **Hirex – Tool, Plant & Equipment Hire Exhibition**
*Venue:* NEC, Birmingham. *Organizer:* EMAP Business Communications. 0171 388 2430

Jan 29–30     **LAMMA – Lincolnshire Agricultural Machinery Manufacturing Exhibition**
*Venue:* Showground, Lincoln. *Organizer:* LAMMA. 01522 750327

Mar 19–20     **Midlands Manufacturing**
*Venue:* NEC, Birmingham. *Organizer:* European Trade & Exhibition Services Ltd. 01784 880890

Apr 22–24   **Traffex 97 – Int'l Traffic Engineering & Road Safety Exhibition**
            *Venue:* NEC, Birmingham. *Organizer:* Printerhall. 0171 436 7016

## Farming/Agricultural

Jan 29–30   **LAMMA – Lincolnshire Agricultural Machinery Manufacturing Exhibition**
            *Venue:* Showground, Lincoln. *Organizer:* LAMMA. 01522 750327

Feb 5–6     **Grain 97**
            *Venue:* NAC Stoneleigh Park, Warwickshire. *Organizer:* Royal Agricultural Soci-
            ety of England. 01203 535712

Apr 9–10    **Muck 97**
            *Venue:* NAC Stoneleigh Park, Warwickshire. *Organizer:* Royal Agricultural Soci-
            ety of England. 01203 535712

May 11      **Grasslands South West**
            *Venue:* The Showground, Shepton Mallet. *Organizer:* Royal Bath & West of Eng-
            land Society. 01749 822200

May 14–15   **British Pig & Poultry Show**
            *Venue:* NAC Stoneleigh Park, Warwickshire. *Organizer:* Royal Agricultural Soci-
            ety of England. 01203 535712

May 16–17   **Shropshire & West Midlands Show**
            *Venue:* The Showground, Shrewsbury. *Organizer:* Shropshire & West Midlands
            Agricultural Society. 01743 362824

Jun 18–19   **Cheshire County Show**
            *Venue:* County Showground, Knutsford. *Organizer:* Cheshire Agricultural Soci-
            ety. 01829 760020

Oct 1       **South West Dairy Show**
            *Venue:* The Showground, Shepton Mallet. *Organizer:* Royal Bath & West of Eng-
            land Society. 01749 822200

Nov 27      **Dairy Scot**
            *Venue:* Royal Highland Centre, Edinburgh. *Organizer:* National Farmers Union
            Scotland. 0131 335 3111

## Finance/Insurance/Banking/Law

May 8–9     **National Association of Pension Funds Conference & Exhibition**
            *Venue:* Int'l Exhibition Centre, Harrogate. *Organizer:* NAPF– National Associa-
            tion of Pension Funds. 0171 730 0585

Jun 10–12   **Chartered Institute of Professional Financial Advisers Conference & Exhibition**
            *Venue:* Int'l Exhibition Centre, Harrogate. *Organizer:* CIPFA – Chartered Institute
            of Professional Financial Advisers. 0171 543 5600

## Freighting/Transport

Apr 22–24   **APLS 97 – Advanced Procurement & Logistics Systems Conference & Exhibition.**
            *Venue:* New Connaught Rooms, London. *Organizer:* Applied Network Research
            Ltd. 0181 947 2684

May 14–16   **IRTE 97 – Road Transport Engineering Conference & Exhibition**
            *Venue:* Int'l Centre, Telford. *Organizer:* Institute of Road Transport Engineers.
            0171 630 1111

Oct 2–5     **Logistics Exhibition**
            *Venue:* Oriana, Southampton Dock. *Organizer:* Richmond Events Ltd. 0181 332
            2422

Oct 9–11    **Coach & Bus 97**
            *Venue:* NEC, Birmingham. *Organizer:* Confederation of Passenger Transport UK.
            0171 831 7546

Oct 21–24    **Int'l Handllng & Storage Exhibition**
             *Venue:* NEC, Birmingham. *Organizer:* DMG Trinity Ltd. 01895 677677
Nov 11–13    **Ralltex 97 – 3rd Int'l Products & Services for Railways Exhibition**
             *Venue:* Wembley, London. *Organizer:* Mack–Brooks Exhibitions Ltd. 01707
             275641

## Government/Defence/Education

Jan 23–25    **Job Scene Merseyside**
             *Venue:* St George's Hall, Liverpool. *Organizer:* T J W Exhibitions Ltd. 01823
             433933
Feb 21–22    **Job Scene South West**
             *Venue:* The Pavilions, Plymouth. *Organizer:* T J W Exhibitions Ltd. 01823 433933
Mar 2–4      **Job Scene**
             *Venue:* Docklands Arena, London. *Organizer:* T J W Exhibitions Ltd. 01823
             433933
Mar 2–4      **The Daily Telegraph Graduate Recruitment Fair**
             *Venue:* London Arena, London. *Organizer:* T J W Exhibitions Ltd. 01823 433933
Mar 6–8      **The Education Show 97**
             *Venue:* NEC, Birmingham. *Organizer:* EMAP Business Communications. 0171
             388 2430
Jun 10–12    **National Town Planning Exhibition**
             *Venue:* ICC, Edinburgh. *Organizer:* Royal Town Planning Institute. 0171 636 9107
Jul 4–5      **Education South West**
             *Venue:* Westpoint Centre, Exeter. *Organizer:* British Educational Supplies Associ-
             ation. 0171 537 4997
Jul 10–11    **Training & Enterprise Council Conference & Exhibition**
             *Venue:* Metropole Hotel, Birmingham. *Organizer:* Touchstone Exhibitions & Con-
             ferences Ltd. 0181 332 0044
Sep 30–Oct 1 **Education Northern Ireland 97**
             *Venue:* King's Hall, Belfast. *Organizer:* British Educational Supplies Association.
             0171 537 4997

## Hardware/Do It Yourself

Jan 19–21    **The DIY & Home Improvement Show**
             *Venue:* Olympia, London. *Organizer:* First Events & Conferences. 0181 462 0721

## Health/Medicine

Mar DTBA     **Naidex Int'l – Int'l Aids for the Disabled & Elderly Exhibition**
             *Venue:* NEC, Birmingham. *Organizer:* Reed Exhibition Company UK. 0181 910
             7910
Mar DTBA     **Scottish Naidex – Aids for the Disabled & Elderly Exhibition**
             *Venue:* SECC, Glasgow. *Organizer:* Richmond Events Ltd. 0181 332 2422
Mar 4–6      **Safety & Health at Work Exhibition 97**
             *Venue:* Earls Court, London. *Organizer:* Paramount Exhibitions & Conferences.
             0181 207 5599
Apr 9–11     **Association of Surgeons of GB & Ireland Annual Meeting & Exhibition**
             *Venue:* Int'l Centre, Bournemouth. *Organizer:* Event Presentations Ltd. 01483
             426608
Apr 19–21    **Optrafair 97 – Ophthalmic Trade Fair**
             *Venue:* NEC, Birmingham. *Organizer:* Ophthalmic Exhibitors Association. 0171
             405 8101

| | |
|---|---|
| Apr 24–26 | **Int'l Dental Showcase 97**<br>*Venue:* NEC, Birmingham. *Organizer:* British Dental Trade Association. 01494 431010 |
| May 9–10 | **General Practice 97 Conference & Exhibition**<br>*Venue:* NEC, Birmingham. *Organizer:* Sterling Events. 0151 709 8979 |
| May 19–21 | **Med X Ray Exhibition**<br>*Venue:* Birmingham. *Organizer:* British Institute of Radiology. 0171 580 4085 |
| May 19–21 | **Radiology 97**<br>*Venue:* ICC, Birmingham. *Organizer:* British Institute of Radiology. 0171 580 4085 |
| May 20–22 | **British Cardiac Society Annual Meeting & Exhibition**<br>*Venue:* G-Mex, Manchester. *Organizer:* Event Presentations Ltd. 01483 426608 |
| Jun DTBA | **Northern Naidex 97 – National Aids for the Disabled & Elderly Exhibition**<br>*Venue:* Exhibition Centre, Doncaster. *Organizer:* Richmond Events Ltd. 0181 332 2422 |
| Sep 24–26 | **British Orthopaedic Association Annual Meeting & Exhibition**<br>*Venue:* Int'l Arena, Cardiff. *Organizer:* Event Presentations Ltd. 01483 426608 |
| Oct 7–9 | **National Association of Theatre Nurses Annual Conference & Exhibition 97**<br>*Venue:* Int'l Centre, Harrogate. *Organizer:* National Association of Theatre Nurses. |

## Marine/Aviation

| | |
|---|---|
| Jan 3–12 | **London Int'l Boat Show**<br>*Venue:* Earls Court, London. *Organizer:* BMIF, The. 01784 473377 |
| Mar 1–2 | **Sailboat – The RYA National Dinghy Show**<br>*Venue:* Alexandra Palace, London. *Organizer:* Royal Yachting Association. 01703 627425 |
| May 13–15 | **Cruise & Ferry 97**<br>*Venue:* Olympia, London. *Organizer:* BML Business Meetings Ltd. 01923 776363 |
| Jun 1–6 | **Int'l Association of Ports & Harbours**<br>*Venue:* Hilton, London. *Organizer:* Concorde Services Ltd. 0181 743 3106 |
| Oct 7–10 | **Imdex Europe – Int'l Maritime Defence Conference & Exhibition**<br>*Venue:* National Maritime Museum, London. *Organizer:* Spearhead Exhibitions Ltd. 0181 949 9222 |

## Materials/Packaging/Processing

| | |
|---|---|
| Mar 4–6 | **Fast 97 – Finishing & Surface Technology Exhibition**<br>*Venue:* Exhibition Centre, Telford. *Organizer:* Turret Group plc. 01923 228577 |
| Mar 19–20 | **Midlands Manufacturing**<br>*Venue:* NEC, Birmingham. *Organizer:* European Trade & Exhibition Services Ltd. 01784 880890 |
| Apr 15–17 | **Foodpak – 3rd Northern Ireland Food Packaging Exhibition**<br>*Venue:* King's Hall, Belfast. *Organizer:* Industrial & Trade Exhibitions. 01232 230425 |
| Apr 22–24 | **Solidex**<br>*Venue:* Exhibition Centre, Harrogate. *Organizer:* DMG Trinity Ltd. 01895 677677 |
| Jun 6–7 | **Far West Materials Handling 97**<br>*Venue:* Westpoint Centre, Exeter. *Organizer:* Westpoint Centre. 01392 444777 |
| Oct 14–16 | **Papex – Int'l Pul & Paper Conference & Exhibition**<br>*Venue:* G-Mex, Manchester. *Organizer:* Reed Exhibition Company Ltd. 0121 705 6707 |
| Oct 21–24 | **IHSE 97 – Int'l Handling & Storage Exhibition**<br>*Venue:* NEC, Birmingham. Organizer; DMG Trinity Ltd. 01895 677677 |

Nov DTBA     **Manufacturing Week 97**
*Venue:* NEC, Birmingham. *Organizer:* Reed Exhibition Company UK. 0181 910 7910

Nov DTBA     **Rapid Prototyping & Tooling Exhibition**
*Venue:* NEC, Birmingham. *Organizer:* Reed Exhibition Company UK. 0181 910 7910

Nov 25–27     **World of Concrete Europe 97**
*Venue:* NEC, Birmingham. *Organizer:* Westrade Group. 01923 778311

### Mining/Metals

Jun 9–13     **18th Int'l Galvanizing Conference & Exhibition**
*Venue:* ICC, Birmingham. *Organizer:* Concorde Services Ltd. 0181 743 3106

Jun 24–26     **Hillhead 97 – Quarrying and Heavy Construction Equipment Exhibition**
*Venue:* Hillhead Quarry, Buxton. *Organizer:* Quarry Management. 0115 941 1315

Sep 2–4     **Tunnelling 97**
*Venue:* Olympia, London. *Organizer:* Institution of Mining & Metals. 0171 580 3802

### Petroleum/Chemicals

May 20–22     **Laboratory 97**
*Venue:* Earls Court, London. *Organizer:* Reed Exhibition Company UK. 0181 910 7910

Jun 1–2     **Forecourt Show, Forecourt Shop & Convenience Retailing Exhibition 97**
*Venue:* NEC, Birmingham. *Organizer:* Blenheim Group plc. 0181 742 2828

Jun 4–6     **Chlorine 97**
*Venue:* London. *Organizer:* Society of Chemical Industry. 0171 235 3681

Jun 11–12     **Chemical Specialities Europe 97**
*Venue:* G-Mex, Manchester. *Organizer:* FMJ International Publications Ltd. 01737 768611

### Printing/Photography/Books

Mar DTBA     **Scotprint 97**
*Venue:* Gleneagles. *Organizer:* Trade Exhibiions Scotland. 01786 880255

Mar 16–18     **Book Print London**
*Venue:* Olympia, London. *Organizer:* Pams Group.01708 340059

Mar 16–18     **London International Book Fair**
*Venue:* Olympia, London. *Organizer:* Reed Exhibition Company UK. 0181 910 7910

Apr 14–16     **Newstec 97**
*Venue:* Metropole, Brighton. *Organizer:* Pattenden Trade Fairs. 01203 644200

Apr 19–20     **Pro–Am Photo – Photographic Exhibition**
*Venue:* G-Mex, Manchester. *Organizer:* Top Events Ltd. 01829 770884

Jun 27–29     **Under One Umbrella Four – 4th Librarians & Information Specialists Biennial Meeting & Exhibition**
*Venue:* UMIST Campus, Manchester. *Organizer:* Library Association. 0171 636 7543

Jul 1–2     **Magazine Publishing 97 Exhibition**
*Venue:* Olympia, London. *Organizer:* Legend Communications Ltd. 0181 240 4444

Oct 14–16     **Papex – Pulp & Paper Conference & Exhibition**
*Venue:* G-Mex, Manchester. *Organizer:* Reed Exhibition Company Ltd. 0121 705 6707

Oct 18–21    **PMA Europe 97 – Photographic Exhibition**
*Venue:* Olympia, London. *Organizer:* Photo Marketing Association International
UK Ltd. 0121 212 0299

## Property/Real Estate

Jan 24–25    **French Property Exhibition**
*Venue:* Novotel, London. *Organizer:* French Property News. 0181 944 5500

Feb 22–23    **Lincolnshire Ideal Home Exhibition & Wedding Show**
*Venue:* Lincolnshire Showground, Lincolnshire. *Organizer:* Taylor Robinson
Associates Ltd. 01476 594954

Mar 7–9    **Emigration 97 Show**
*Venue:* Olympia, London. *Organizer:* Homebuyer Events Ltd. 0181 877 3636

Mar 7–9    **The Evening Standard Homebuyer Show**
*Venue:* Olympia, London. *Organizer:* Homebuyer Events Ltd. 0181 877 3636

Mar 13–Apr 6    **The Daily Mail Ideal Home Exhibition**
*Venue:* Earls Court, London. *Organizer:* DMG Trinity Ltd. 01895 677677

## Purchasing/Retailing

Jan 18–19    **Brides 97**
*Venue:* Int'l Exhibition Centre, Telford. *Organizer:* S.S.R. TV Associates. 01743
260000

Jan 23–26    **The Glasgow Trade Fair**
*Venue:* SECC, Glasgow. *Organizer:* Made in Scotland Ltd. 01463 782578

Jan 25–26    **London Bridal Fair**
*Venue:* Alexandra Palace. *Organizer:* National Bridal Fairs. 01423 530588

Jan 31–Feb 2    **Wedding Exhibition**
*Venue:* Int'l Centre, Bournemouth. *Organizer:* Bournemouth International Centre.
01202 552122

Feb 2–6    **ISF – Int'l Spring Fair**
*Venue:* NEC, Birmingham. *Organizer:* Trade Promotion Services Ltd. 0181 855
9201

Feb 6–9    **National Wedding Show**
*Venue:* Olympia, London. *Organizer:* Wedding Shows UK Ltd. 01462 485881

Feb 16–18    **Premier Collections 97**
*Venue:* NEC, Birmingham. *Organizer:* Blenheim Group plc. 0181 742 2828

Feb 16–19    **Scottish Bridal & Fashion**
*Venue:* Moat House Hotel, Glasgow. *Organizer:* Trade Exhibitions Scotland. 01786
880255

Feb 16–19    **Scottish Spring Fair**
*Venue:* SECC, Glasgow. *Organizer:* Trade Exhibitions Scotland. 01786 880255

Feb 22–23    **Lincolnshire Ideal Home Exhibition & Wedding Show**
*Venue:* Lincolnshire Showground, Lincolnshire. *Organizer:* Taylor Robinson
Associates Ltd. 01476 594954

Mar 11–13    **Intershop 97**
*Venue:* Olympia, London. *Organizer:* Montgomery Exhibitions Ltd. 0171 486
1951

Mar 11–13    **POP Expo 97 – Point of Purchase Exhibition**
*Venue:* Olympia, London. *Organizer:* Montgomery Exhibitions Ltd. 0171 486
1951

Mar 11–13    **Retail Construct 97**
*Venue:* Olympia, London. *Organizer:* Montgomery Exhibitions Ltd. 0171 486
1951

May 20–22    **Retail Solutions 97**
*Venue:* NEC, Birmingham. *Organizer:* EMAP Maclaren. 0181 277 5346

Jun 1–2    **Forecourt Show, Forecourt Shop & Convenience Retailing Exhibition 97**
*Venue:* NEC, Birmingham. *Organizer:* Blenheim Group plc. 0181 742 2828

Jun 5–8    **The Country Style Fair 97**
*Venue:* NEC, Birmingham. *Organizer:* Orchard Events Ltd. 0181 742 2020

Jun 29–Jul 2    **National Accessory & Luggage Fair**
*Venue:* National Motorcycle Museum, Birmingham. *Organizer:* M & S Management Services. 0161 437 1943

Aug DTBA    **Premier Collections 97**
*Venue:* NEC, Birmingham. *Organizer:* Blenheim Group plc. 0181 742 2828

Aug 31–Sep 2    **Premier Menswear London**
*Venue:* Olympia, London. *Organizer:* Blenheim Group plc. 0181 742 2828

Sep DTBA    **Int'l Jewellery London**
*Venue:* Earls Court, London. *Organizer:* Reed Exhibition Company UK. 0181 910 7910

## Radio/Television/Video

Feb 18–20    **Video Forum 97**
*Venue:* Wembley, London. *Organizer:* VCM Communications. 01273 857800

Mar 12–14    **The Television Show**
*Venue:* Business Design Centre, London. *Organizer:* IIR Industrial Ltd. 0171 412 0141

May 4    **National Vintage Communications Fair**
*Venue:* Wembley, London. *Organizer:* Jonathon Hill (Sunrise Press). 01398 331532

## Recreation/Sports/Hobbies

Jan 7–10    **Autosport International**
*Venue:* NEC, Birmingham. *Organizer:* Haymarket Exhibitions Ltd. 0171 402 2555

Jan 10–12    **Adventure Travel & Sports Show**
*Venue:* Olympia, London. *Organizer:* PA Show Management. 01795 844939

Jan 21–23    **Int'l Amusement Trade Exhibition**
*Venue:* Earls Court, London. *Organizer:* Amusement Trade Exhibitions Ltd. 0171 713 0302

Jan 21–23    **Int'l Casino Exhibition**
*Venue:* Earls Court, London. *Organizer:* Amusement Trade Exhibitions Ltd. 0171 713 0302

Jan 22–24    **BIGGA Turf Management Exhibition**
*Venue:* Int'l Centre, Harrogate. *Organizer:* BIGGA – British & Int'l Golf Green Keepers Association. 01347 838581

Jan 23–26    **Caravan, Leisure & Home Show**
*Venue:* G-Mex, Manchester. *Organizer:* P&O Events Limited. 0171 244 6433

Jan 30–Feb 2    **Road Racing & Superbike Show**
*Venue:* Alexandra Palace, London. *Organizer:* Shire PR & Marketing Ltd. 01440 707055

Jan 31–Feb 2    **Holiday & Leisure Exhibition**
*Venue:* Winter Gardens, Blackpool. *Organizer:* Evening Gazette. 01253 831024

Feb 5–9    **Outdoors 97 – Scotland's Premier Leisure Event**
*Venue:* SECC, Glasgow. *Organizer:* Eventex. 0141 204 0123

Mar DTBA    **Scottish Sports Trade Show 97**
*Venue:* Gleneagles. *Organizer:* Trade Exhibitions Scotland. 01786 880255

Mar 2–4      **Spring COLA – Camping & Outdoor Leisure Exhibition**
             *Venue:* Int'l Centre, Harrogate. *Organizer:* COLA–Camping & Outdoor Leisure
             Association. 0181 842 1111
Mar 2–5      **Soltex 97 – Outdoor Leisure Trade Exhibition**
             *Venue:* G-Mex, Manchester. *Organizer:* British Ski Federation. 01506 884943
Mar 11–13    **Recman – Sports & Leisure Facilities Conference & Exhibition**
             *Venue:* NEC, Birmingham. *Organizer:* Blenheim Group plc. 0181 742 2828
Apr 8–10     **AVEX 97 – Sports & Leisure Exhibition**
             *Venue:* NEC, Birmingham. *Organizer:* AVAB. 01737 357211

## Safety/Security

Jan 14–16    **Securex 97**
             *Venue:* Olympia, London. *Organizer:* Paramount Exhibitions & Conferences.
             0181 207 5599
Mar 4–6      **Safety & Health at Work Exhibition 97**
             *Venue:* Earls Court, London. *Organizer:* Paramount Exhibitions & Conferences.
             0181 207 5599
Apr DTBA     **Infosec 97 – Information Security Exhibition**
             *Venue:* Olympia, London. *Organizer:* Reed Exhibition Company UK. 0181 910
             7910
May 12–15    **IFSEC – Int'l Fire & Security Exhibition**
             *Venue:* NEC, Birmingham. *Organizer:* Blenheim Group plc. 0181 742 2828
May 12–15    **Int'l Firex – Fire Protection & Safety Exhibition**
             *Venue:* NEC, Birmingham. *Organizer:* Blenheim Group plc. 0181 742 2828

## Science/Technology

Jan 17–18    **Winter Scientific Meeting & Technical Exhibition**
             *Venue:* QEII Conference Centre, London. *Organizer:* Association of Anaesthetists
             of GB & Ireland. 0171 631 1650
Mar 28–30    **Physics World Exhibition**
             *Venue:* Leeds University, Leeds. *Organizer:* Institute of Physics. 0171 470 4800
May 13–15    **Technology Transfer 97**
             *Venue:* NEC, Birmingham. *Organizer:* Miller Freeman Exhibitions (UK) Ltd. 0181
             302 8585
May 20–22    **Laboratory 97**
             *Venue:* Earls Court, London. *Organizer:* Reed Exhibition Company UK. 0181 910
             7910
Sep 10–12    **Annual Scientific Meeting & Technical Exhibition**
             *Venue:* Harrogate. *Organizer:* Association of Anaesthetists of GB & Ireland. 0171
             631 1650
Oct 1–2      **Scientific Computing Exhibition**
             *Venue:* Sandown Exhibition Centre, Esher. *Organizer:* Institute of Physics. 0171
             470 4800

## Textiles/Clothing

Jan 16–Jul 19  **The Knitting, Needlecraft & Design Exhibition**
               *Venue:* Sandown Exhibition Centre, Esher. *Organizer:* Nationwide Exhibitions
               UK Ltd. 0117 970 1370
Jan 18–19      **Brides 97**
               *Venue:* Int'l Exhibition Centre, Telford. *Organizer:* S.S.R. TV Associates. 01743
               260000

Jan 25–26    **London Bridal Fair**
*Venue:* Alexandra Palace. *Organizer:* National Bridal Fairs. UK. 01423 530588

Jan 31–Feb 2    **Wedding Exhibition**
*Venue:* Int'l Centre, Bournemouth. *Organizer:* Bournemouth International Centre. 01202 552122

Feb 6–9    **National Wedding Show**
*Venue:* Olympia, London. *Organizer:* Wedding Shows UK Ltd. 01462 485881

Feb 16–18    **Premier Collections 97**
*Venue:* NEC, Birmingham. *Organizer:* Blenheim Group plc. 0181 742 2828

Feb 16–19    **Scottish Bridal & Fashion**
*Venue:* Moat House Hotel, Glasgow. *Organizer:* Trade Exhibitions Scotland. 01786 880255

Feb 20–23    **The North West Knitting & Needlecraft Exhibition**
*Venue:* G-Mex, Manchester. *Organizer:* Nationwide Exhibitions UK Ltd. 0117 970 1370

Feb 22–23    **Lincolnshire Ideal Home Exhibition & Wedding Show**
*Venue:* Lincolnshire Showground, Lincolnshire. *Organizer:* Taylor Robinson Associates Ltd. 01476 594954

Apr 11–13    **The North East Knitting & Needlecraft Exhibition**
*Venue:* University Exhibition Centre, Leeds. *Organizer:* National Association for Special Educational Needs. 01827 311500

Jun 5–8    **The Country Style Fair 97**
*Venue:* NEC, Birmingham. *Organizer:* Orchard Events Ltd. 0181 742 2020

Aug DTBA    **Premier Collections 97**
*Venue:* NEC, Birmingham. *Organizer:* Blenheim Group plc. 0181 742 2828

Aug 31–Sep 2    **Premier Menswear London**
*Venue:* Olympia, London. *Organizer:* Blenheim Group plc. 0181 742 2828


### Travel/Timesharing

Jan 10–12    **Adventure Travel & Sports Show**
*Venue:* Olympia, London. *Organizer:* PA Show Management. 01795 844939

Jan 10–12    **The Holiday Show**
*Venue:* G-Mex, Manchester. *Organizer:* John Fish Exhibitions Ltd. 0115 967 9379

Jan 18–19    **Cheltenham International Holiday Show**
*Venue:* Town Hall, Cheltenham. *Organizer:* Premier Exhibitions. 01242 516738

Jan 24–26    **Independent Travellers World**
*Venue:* Royal Horticultural Halls, London. *Organizer:* Independent Travellers World. 0117 908 3300

Jan 31–Feb 2    **Bournemouth International Holiday Show**
*Venue:* Int'l Centre, Bournemouth. *Organizer:* Premier Exhibitions. 01242 516738

Jan 31–Feb 2    **Holiday & Leisure Exhibition**
*Venue:* Winter Gardens, Blackpool. *Organizer:* Evening Gazette. 01253 831024

Jan 31–Feb 2    **Interhol 97**
*Venue:* Int'l Centre, Bournemouth. *Organizer:* Pressex Promotions. 01543 686942

Feb 6–9    **Destinations 97**
*Venue:* Olympia, London. *Organizer:* Consumer Exhibitions. 0181 948 1666

Feb 8–9    **Brighton International Holiday Show**
*Venue:* Brighton Centre, Brighton. *Organizer:* Premier Exhibitions. 01242 516738

Feb 12–14    **Business Travel 97**
*Venue:* Business Design Centre, London. *Organizer:* Centaur Exhibitions. 0171 287 5678

Mar 7–9   **Emigration 97 Show**
          *Venue:* Olympia, London. *Organizer:* Homebuyer Events Ltd. 0181 877 3636
Mar 19–20 **British Travel Trade Fair 97**
          *Venue:* NEC, Bimmingham. *Organizer:* Reed Exhibition Company UK. 0181 910 7910
Apr 29–30 **Travel International**
          *Venue:* NEC, Birmingham. *Organizer:* Trade Exhibitions Scotland. 01786 880255
May 13–15 **Cruise & Ferry 97**
          *Venue:* Olympia, London. *Organizer:* BML Business Meetings Ltd. 01923 776363
Nov 17–20 **World Travel Market Show**
          *Venue:* Earls Court, London. *Organizer:* Reed Exhibition Company UK. 0181 910 7910

## Wildlife/Pets

Jan 1–2   **Cage Bird Society Show**
          *Venue:* Royal Highland Centre, Edinburgh. *Organizer:* Royal Highland Centre. 0131 333 3036
Jan 12    **The Capital Show – London Racing Pigeon Show**
          *Venue:* Royal Horticultural Halls, London. *Organizer:* Rick Osman. 0171 833 5959
Feb 23–25 **Beta International**
          *Venue:* NEC Birmingham. *Organizer:* BETA – British Equestrian Trade 0113 289 2267
Mar 6–9   **Crufts Dog Show**
          *Venue:* NEC, Birmingham. *Organizer:* Kennel Club. 0171 493 7838
Apr 3–6   **Small Animal Veterinary Exhibition**
          *Venue:* ICC, Birmingham. *Organizer:* BSAVA. 01242 862994
Apr 20–21 **Petindex 97**
          *Venue:* NEC, Birmingham. *Organizer:* Dog World Publications/Pet Trade & Industry Association. 01233 621877

## Wines/Spirits/Brewing

Feb 9–13  **IFE 97 – Int'l Food & Drink Exhibition**
          *Venue:* Earls Court, London. *Organizer:* Andry Montgomery Ltd. 0171 486 1951
Feb 16–18 **British Drinks Week**
          *Venue:* NEC, Birmingham. *Organizer:* Trades Exhibitions Ltd. 0171 610 3001
Feb 18–20 **National Pub Trade Exhibition**
          *Venue:* Sheffield Arena, Sheffield. *Organizer:* Complete Events Management Ltd. 01425 461561
Mar 17–20 **Scothot 97 – 13th Scottish Hotel, Catering & Licensed Trade Exhibition**
          *Venue:* SECC, Glasgow. *Organizer:* Scottish Industrial & Trade Exhibitions Ltd. 0131 556 5152
Mar 18–19 **Wine Scotland 97 – 3rd Wine & Spirit Show**
          *Venue:* SECC, Glasgow. *Organizer:* Scottish Industrial & Trade Exhibitions Ltd. 0131 556 5152
Apr 15–17 **NIFEX 97 – 6th Northern Ireland Int'l Food, Drink & Catering Exhibition**
          *Venue:* Kings Hall, Belfast. *Organizer:* Industrial Trade Exhibitions 01232 230425
Apr 18–19 **The Sunday Times Wine Club Vintage Festival**
          *Venue:* Royal Horticultural Halls, London. *Organizer:* Sunday Times Wine Club. 01734 481713
Apr 22–24 **Food & Drink Processing 97**
          *Venue:* Olympia, London. *Organizer:* Reed Exhibition Company UK. 0181 910 7910

Jun 28–29    **Cyprus Wine Festival**
             *Venue:* Alexandra Palace, London. *Organizer:* Parikiaki. 0171 272 6777

**Women/Home/Gardening**

Jan 16–Jul 19  **The Knitting, Needlecraft & Design Exhibition**
             *Venue:* Sandown Exhibition Centre, Esher. *Organizer:* Nationwide Exhibitions
             UK Ltd. 0117 970 1370

Jan 18–19    **Brides 97**
             *Venue:* Int'l Exhibition Centre, Telford. *Organizer:* S.S.R. TV Associates. 01743
             260000

Jan 18–22    **Decorative Interiors 97**
             *Venue:* NEC, Birmingham. *Organizer:* Blenheim Group plc. 0181 742 2828

Jan 19–21    **The DIY & Home Improvement Show**
             *Venue:* Olympia, London. *Organizer:* First Events & Conferences. 0181 462 0721

Jan 19–22    **KBB 97 – Fitted Furniture, Decorative Interiors & Appliances Exhibition**
             *Venue:* NEC, Birmingham. *Organizer:* Blenheim Group plc. 0181 742 2828

Jan 19–22    **The Furniture Show 97 – Incorporating Lighting & Furnishing Accessories**
             *Venue:* NEC, Birmingham. *Organizer:* Blenheim Group plc. 0181 742 2828

Jan 22–24    **BIGGA Turf Management Exhibition**
             *Venue:* Int'l Centre, Harrogate. *Organizer:* BIGGA – British & Int'l Golf Green
             Keepers Association. 01347 838581

Jan 23–26    **Caravan, Leisure & Home Show**
             *Venue:* G-Mex, Manchester. *Organizer:* P&O Events Limited. 0171 244 6433

Jan 23–26    **The Glasgow Trade Fair**
             *Venue:* SECC, Glasgow. *Organizer:* Made in Scotland Ltd. 01463 782578

Jan 25–26    **London Bridal Fair**
             *Venue:* Alexandra Palace. *Organizer:* National Bridal Fairs. 01423 530588

Jan 31–Feb 2  **Wedding Exhibition**
             *Venue:* Int'l Centre, Bournemouth. *Organizer:* Bournemouth International Cen-
             tre. 01202 552122

Feb 6–9      **National Wedding Show**
             *Venue:* Olympia, London. *Organizer:* Wedding Shows UK Ltd. 01462 485881

Feb 16–18    **Premier Collections 97**
             *Venue:* NEC, Birmingham. *Organizer:* Blenheim Group plc. 0181 742 2828

Feb 16–19    **Scottish Bridal & Fashion**
             *Venue:* Moat House Hotel, Glasgow. *Organizer:* Trade Exhibitions Scotland.
             01786 880255

Feb 16–19    **Scottish Spring Fair**
             *Venue:* SECC, Glasgow. *Organizer:* Trade Exhibitions Scotland. 01786 880255

Feb 18–19    **BGLA 97 – British Growers Look Ahead 97**
             *Venue:* NEC, Bimmingham. *Organizer:* BGLA Ltd. 0171 235 5077

Feb 20–23    **The North West Knitting & Needlecraft Exhibition**
             *Venue:* G-Mex, Manchester. *Organizer:* Nationwide Exhibitions UK Ltd. 0117
             970 1370

Feb 22–23    **Lincolnshire Ideal Home Exhibition & Wedding Show**
             *Venue:* Lincolnshire Showground, Lincolnshire. *Organizer:* Taylor Robinson
             Associates Ltd. 01476 594954

Mar 4–9      **The Country Living Fair**
             *Venue:* Business Design Centre, London. *Organizer:* Business Design Centre.
             0171 359 3535

Mar 7–9      **The Evening Standard Homebuyer Show**
             *Venue:* Olympia, London. *Organizer:* Homebuyer Events Ltd. 0181 877 3636

Mar 13–Apr 6  **The Daily Mail Ideal Home Exhibition**
*Venue:* Earls Court, London. *Organizer:* DMG Trinity Ltd. 01895 677677

Mar 21–23  **50 Plus Lifestyle Show**
*Venue:* Exhibition Centre, Aberdeen. *Organizer:* Third Age Events Ltd. 01483 2723025

Mar 23–25  **Harrogate Nursery Fair**
*Venue:* Int'l Centre, Harrogate. *Organizer:* Harrogate Pram Fairs Ltd. 01902 671974

Apr 11–13  **The North East Knitting & Needlecraft Exhibition**
*Venue:* University Exhibition Centre, Leeds. *Organizer:* National Association for Special Educational Needs. 01827 311500

Apr 24–27  **Spring Flower Show**
*Venue:* Gt Yorkshire Showground, Harrogate. *Organizer:* North of England Horticultural Society. 01423 561049

May 21–22  **Living in Britain Conference & Exhibition**
*Venue:* Duke of York HQ, London. *Organizer:* First Event Ltd. 0171 252 7459

Jun 5–8  **The Country Style Fair 97**
*Venue:* NEC, Birmingham. *Organizer:* Orchard Events Ltd. 0181 742 2020

Aug DTBA  **Premier Collections 97**
*Venue:* NEC, Birmingham. *Organizer:* Blenheim Group plc. 0181 742 2828

Aug 31–Sep 2  **Premier Menswear London**
*Venue:* Olympia, London. *Organizer:* Blenheim Group plc. 0181 742 2828

Sep 12–14  **Great Autumn Flower Show**
*Venue:* Gt Yorkshire Showground, Harrogate. *Organizer:* North of England Horticultural Society. 01423 561049

Nov 28–30  **The Festive Table**
*Venue:* Alexandra Palace, London. *Organizer:* Marathon Event Management. 0181 366 3153

Nov 29–30  **National Christmas Lacemakers Fair**
*Venue:* NEC, Birmingham. *Organizer:* John Jennifer Ford. 01543 491000

Please note that this appendix is based on selected extracts from *Conferences and Exhibitions Diary* – see Appendix E: Recommended Reading, page 137. Information is reproduced with the permission of the publisher, Themetree Limited.

Details are believed to be correct as at 1 November 1996 but are liable to change. You may wish to subscribe to *Conferences and Exhibitions Diary* for further information and regular updates.

Inclusion within this appendix does not necessarily constitute a recommendation for the exhibitions listed and you should take sensible precautions and professional advice before entering into business arrangements with the organizers.

# Appendix B: Exhibition organizers

Amusement Trade Exhibitions Ltd, Regency Wharf, 6 All Saints Street, London, N1 9RQ. 0171 713 0302

Andry Montgomery Ltd, 11 Manchester Square, London, W1M 5AB. 0171 486 1951

Applied Network Research Ltd, Research House, Lancaster Avenue, London, SW19 5DE. 0181 947 2684

AR Trade Fairs Ltd, Suite 6, Mostyn Hall, Friargate, Penrith, Cumbria CA11 7XR. 01768 899739

Association of Anaesthetists of GB & Ireland, 9 Bedford Square, London, WC1B 3RA. 0171 631 1650

AVAB, Bassett House, High Street, Banstead, Surrey, SM7 2LZ. 01737 357211

BETA – British Equestrian Trade Association, Wothersome Grange, Bramham, Wetherby, West Yorks, LS23 6LY. 0113 289 2267

BGLA Ltd, Agriculture House, Knightsbridge, London, SW1X 7NJ. 0171 235 5077

BIGGA – British & Int'l Golf Green Keepers Association, Aldwalk Manor, Aldwalk, Alme, York, YO6 2NF. 01347 838581

Blenheim Group plc, Blenheim House, 630 Chiswick High Road, London, W4 5BG. 0181 742 2828

BMIF, The, Meadlake Place, Thorpe Lea Road, Egham, Surrey, TW20 8HF. 01784 473377

BML Business Meetings Ltd, 2 Station Road, Rickmansworth, Herts, WD3 1QP. 01923 776363

Bournemouth International Centre, Exeter Road, Bournemouth, BH2 5BH. 01202 552122

Brainstorm Exhibitions Ltd, 4 Market Place, Hertford, Herts, SG14 1EB. 01992 501177

British Dental Trade Association, Merritt House, Hill Avenue, Amersham, Bucks, HP6 5BQ. 01494 431010

British Educational Supplies, Association, 20 Beaufort Court, Admirals Way, London, E14 9XL. 0171 5374997

British Institute of Radiology, 36 Portland Place, London, W1N 4AT. 0171 580 4085

British Ski Federation, 258 Main Street, East Calder, Edinburgh, EH53 0EE. 01506 884943

BSAVA, Kingsley House, Church Lane, Shurdington, Cheltenham, Glos GL5 5TQ. 01242 862994

Business Design Centre, 52 Upper Street, Islington, London, N1 0QH. 0171 359 3535

Business Events Ltd, 100 Wellington Street, Leeds, LS1 4LT. 0113 237 3022

Business Intelligence, Forum House, 1 Graham Road, Wimbledon, London, SW19 3SW. 0181 544 1830

Business Meetings Ltd, 2 Station Road, Rickmansworth, Herts, WD3 1QP. 01923 776363

Centaur Exhibitions, St Giles House, 50 Poland Street, London, W1V 4AX. 0171 287 5678

Cheshire Agricultural Society, Clay Lane Farm, Marton, Winsford, Cheshire, CW7 2QH. 01829 760020

CIPFA – Chartered Institute of Professional Financial Advisers, 3 Robert Street, London, WC2N 6BH. 0171 543 5600

COLA – Camping & Outdoor Leisure Association, Morritt House, 58 Station Approach, South Ruislip, Middlesex, HA4 6SA. 0181 842 1111

Complete Events Management Ltd, Kingsbury House, Fridays Cross Mews, Christchurch Road, Ringwood, Hants, BH24 1DG. 01425 461561

Concorde Services Ltd, 10 Wendell Road, London, W12 9RT. 0181 743 3106

Confederation of Passenger, Transport UK, Sardinia House, 52 Lincolns Inn Fields, London, WC2A 3LZ. 0171 831 7546

Conference Communication, Monks Hill, Tilford, Farnham, Surrey, GU10 2AJ. 01252 783111

Consumer Exhibitions, Greyhound House, 23-24 George Street, Richmond, Surrey, TW9 1 HY. 0181 948 1666

DMG Trinity Ltd, Times House, Station Approach, Ruislip, Middx, HA4 8NB. 01895 677677

Dog World Publications/Pet Trade & Industry Association, 9 Tufton Street, Ashford, Kent, TN23 1QN. 01233 621877

EMAP Business Communications, Greater London House, Hampstead Road, London, NW1 7QZ. 0171 388 2430

EMAP Maclaren, Maclaren House, 19 Scarbrook Road, Croydon, Surrey, CR9 1QH. 0181 277 5346

European Trade & Exhibition Services Ltd, 9–11 High Street, Staines, Middx, TW1 8 4QY. 01784 880890

Evening Gazette, Preston New Road, Blackpool, FY4 4AU. 01253 831024

Event Presentations Ltd, Petworth Road, Witley, Nr. Godalming, Surrey, GU8 5QW. 01483 426608

Eventex, SECC, Glasgow, G3 8YW. 0141 204 0123

First Events & Conferences, Enterprise House, 27 Hastings Road, Bromley, BR2 8NA. 0181 462 0721

FMJ International Publications Ltd, 2 Queensway, Redhill, Surrey, RH1 1QS. 01737 768611

Framework Marketing & Sales, 22 Market Place, Ringwood, Hants, BH24 1AW. 01425 477565

French Property News, 2 Lambton Road, London, SW20 0LR. 0181 944 5500

Greenwoods Exhibitions, PO Box 49, Aylesbury, Bucks, HP22 5AQ. 01296 631181

Harrogate Pram Fairs Ltd, Greenbank, Wolverhampton Road, Sedgley, Dudley, West Midlands, DY3 1QR. 01902 671974

Haymarket Events, 22 Lancaster Gate, London, W2 3LY. 0171 413 4391

Haymarket Exhibitions Ltd, 55 North Wharf Road, London, W2 1LA. 0171 402 2555

Haymarket Publishing Services, 30 Lancaster Gate, London, W2 3LP. 0171 244 8884

Homebuyer Events Ltd, Mantle House, Broomhill Road, London, SW18 4JQ. 0181 877 3636

Ian Thompson Associates, 26 Lloyd Baker Street, London, WC1X 9AU. 0171 833 3373

IEE Conference Services, Savoy Place, London, WC2R 0BL. 0171 344 5478

IIR Industrial Ltd, 28th Floor, Centre Point, 103 New Oxford Street, London, WC1A 1DD. 0171 412 0141

Independent Travellers World, 9 Byron Place, Clifton, Bristol, BS8 1JT. 0117 908 3300

Industrial Trade Exhibitions, 58 Rugby Road, Belfast, BT7 1PT. 01232 230425

Institute of Physics, 76 Portland Place, London, W1N 4M. 0171 470 4800

Institute of Road Transport Engineers, 22 Greencoat Place, London, SW1P 1PR. 0171 630 1111

Institution of Mining & Metals, 44 Portland Place, London, W1 N 4BR. 0171 580 3802

John & Jennifer Ford, October Hill, Upper Longdon, Rugeley, Staffs, WS15 1QB. 01543 491000

John Fish Exhibitions Ltd, Sherwood House, 17 Longacre, Nottingham, NG5 4JS. 0115 967 9379

Jonathon Hill Sunrise Press, 2–4 Brook Street, Bampton, Devon, EX16 9LY. 01398 331532

Kennel Club, 1 Clarges Street, Piccadilly, London, W1Y 8AB. 0171 493 7838

Kingsgate Group, The, 56 Canon Street, Winchester, Hants, SO23 9JW. 01962 860670

LAMMA, 23 Chapel Lane, Nettleham, Lincoln, LN2 2NX. 01522 750327

Legend Communications Ltd, 1a Rathbone Square, Croydon, Surrey, CR0 1AL. 0181 240 4444

Library Association, 7 Ridgemount Street, London, WC1E 7AE. 0171 636 7543

Lighting Association, The, Stafford Park 7, Telford, Shropshire, TF3 3BQ. 01952 290905

London Furniture Show, The, Hofer House, 185 Uxbridge Road, Hampton, Middlesex, TW2 1BN. 0181 941 8000

M & S Management Services, 5 Greenhythe Road, Heald Green, Cheadle, Cheshire, SK8 3NS. 0161 437 1943

Mack-Brooks Exhibitions Ltd, Forum Place, Hatfield, Herts, AL10 0RN. 01707 275641

Made in Scotland Ltd, The Craft Centre, Beauly, Invernesshire, IV4 7EH. 01463 782578

Marathon Event Management, 53 Windmill Hill, Enfield, Middx, EN2 7AE. 0181 366 3153

Miller Freeman Exhibitions (UK) Ltd, Marlow House, 109 Station Road, Sidcup, Kent, DA15 7ET. 0181 302 8585

Montgomery Exhibitions Ltd, 11 Manchester Square, London, W1M 5AB. 0171 486 1951

NAPF – National Association of Pension Funds, 12–18 Grosvenor Gardens, London, SW1W 0DH. 0171 730 0585

National Association for Special Educational Needs, NASEN House, 4/5 Amber Business Village, Amber Close, Amington, Tamworth. 01827 311500

National Association of Theatre Nurses, 22 Mount Parade, Harrogate, HG1 1BV. 01423 508079

National Bridal Fairs, 64 Duchy Road, Harrogate, North Yorks, HG1 2EZ. 01423 530588

National Custom Sports Car Show, The Middle Lodge, Great North Road, Scawthorpe, Doncaster, DN5 7UN. 01302 783584

National Farmers Union Scotland, Rural Centre – West Mains, Ingliston, Newbridge, Midlothian, EH28 8LT. 0131 335 3111

Nationwide Exhibitions UK Ltd, PO Box 20, Fishponds, Bristol, BS16 5QU. 0117 970 1370

Nexus Ltd, Warwick House, Azalea Drive, Swanley, Kent, BR8 8HY. 01322 660070

North of England Horticultural Society, 4A South Park Road, Harrogate, North Yorks, HG1 5QU. 01423 561049

Ophthalmic Exhibitors Association, 37-41 Bedford Row, London, WC1R 4JH. 0171 405 8101

Orchard Events Ltd, 1 Newton Grove, Chiswick, London, W4 1LB. 0181 742 2020

P&O Events Limited, Earls Court Exhibition Centre, Warwick Road, London, SW5 9TA. 0171 244 6433

PA Show Management, Lower Dane, Hartlip, Kent, ME9 7TE. 01795 844939

Pams Group, St Ives House, Faringdon Avenue, Harold Hill, Romford, RM3 8XL. 01708 340059,

Paramount Exhibitions & Conferences, Paramount House, 17-21 Shenley Road, Borehamwood, Herts, WD6 1RT. 0181 207 5599

Parikiaki, 534A Holloway Road, London, N7 6JP. 0171 272 6777

Pattenden Trade Fairs, PO Box 106, Coventry, CV7 9EA. 01203 644200

Photo Marketing Association, International UK Ltd, Peel Place, 50 Carver Street, Hockley, Birmingham, B1 3AS. 0121 212 0299

Positive Projects, Unit 12–13, Ballinderry Road, Lisburn, BT38 2BP. 01846 603803

Premier Exhibitions, 49 Rodney Road, Cheltenham, GL50 1HX. 01242 516738

Premier Exhibitions & Events Ltd, 3 Raymond Avenue, Thornton Heath, Surrey, CR7 7SB. 0181 684 0465

Pressex Promotions, 66 High Street, Chasetown, Walsall, WS7 8XF. 01543 686942

Printerhall, 29 Newman Street, London, W1 P 3PE. 0171 436 7016

Quarry Management, 7 Regent Street, Nottingham, NG1 5BS. 0115 941 1315

Reed Exhibition Company Ltd, Radcliffe House, Blenheim Court, Solihull, West Midlands, B91 2BG. 0121 705 6707

Reed Exhibition Company UK, Oriel House, 26 The Quadrant, Richmond-upon-Thames, Surrey, TW9 1 DL. 0181 910 7910

Richmond Events Ltd, London House, 243–253 Lower Mortlake Road, Richmond, Surrey, TW9 2LS. 0181 332 2422

Rick Osman, Unit 13, 21 Wren Street, London, WC1X 0HF. 0171 833 5959

Royal Agricultural Society of England, Stoneleigh, Kenilworth, Warks, CV8 2LZ. 01203 535712

Royal Bath & West of England Society, The Showground, Shepton Mallet, BA4 6QN. 01749 822200

Royal Highland Centre, Ingliston, Edinburgh, Scotland, DH28 8NF. 0131 333 3036

Royal Town Planning Institute, 26 Portland Place, London, W1 N 4BE. 0171 636 9107

Royal Yachting Association, RYA House, Romsey Road, Eastleigh, Hants, SO50 9YA. 01703 627425

S.P.N. Exhibitions, 172 London Road, Guildford, Surrey, GU1 1XR. 01483 306304

S.S.R. TV Associates, PO Box 100, Shrewsbury, Salop, SY4 4WF. 01743 260000

Scottish Industrial & Trade, Exhibitions Ltd, 10 Blenheim Place, Edinburgh, EH7 5JH. 0131 556 5152

Scottish Motor Trade Association, 3 Palmerston Place, Edinburgh, EH12 5AF. 0131 225 3643

Shire PR & Marketing Ltd, The White House, Little Wratting, Haverhill, CB9 7UD. 01440 707055

Showbusiness Exhibitions Ltd, 1 Premier Trading Estate, Britannia Road, Waltham Cross, Herts, EN8 7RJ. 01992 788887

Shropshire & West Midlands Agricultural Society, PO Box 62, Shrewsbury, SY1 1Z. 01743 362824

Society for Motor Manufacturers & Traders Ltd, Forbes House, Halkin Street, London, SW1X 7DS. 0171 235 7000

Society of Chemical Industry, 14–15 Belgrave Square, London, SW1X 8PS. 0171 235 3681

Southern Enterprise Exhibitions Ltd, 88A West Street, Farnham, Surrey, GU9 7EN. 01252 734383

Spearhead Exhibitions, 11 Kedington Close, Rougham, IP30 9JF. 01359 271311

Spearhead Exhibitions Ltd, Ocean House, 50 Kingston Road, New Malden, Surrey, KT3 3LZ. 0181 949 9222

Sphinx Exhibitions Ltd, 12 Sandbourne Road, Bournemouth, BH4 8JH. 01202 762252

Sterling Events, 62 Hope Street, Liverpool, L1 9BZ. 0151 709 8979

Sunday Times Wine Club, Aquitanine House, Paddock Road, Reading, RG4 0JY. 01734 481713

T J W Exhibitions Ltd, Fry House, Sandhill Park, Bishops Lydeard, Somerset, TA4 3DE. 01823 433933

Taylor Robinson Associates Ltd, Unit 124, Springfield Park, Springfield Road, Grantham, Lincs, NG31 7BG. 01476 594954

Third Age Events Ltd, 50 Smithbrook Kilns, Cranleigh, Surrey, GU6 8JJ. 01483 2723025

Top Events Ltd, PO Box 1008, Chester. 01829 770884

Touchstone Exhibitions & Conferences Ltd, Haleon House, 4 Red Lion Street, Richmond, Surrey, TW9 1 RW. 0181 332 0044

Trade Exhibitions Scotland, Kierallan House, Braco, Dunblane, Perthshire, FK15 9PR. 01786 880255

Trade Promotion Services Ltd, Exhibition House, 6 Warren Lane, London, SE18 6BW. 0181 855 9201

Trades Exhibitions Ltd, 461–465 North End Road, London, SW6 1 NZ. 0171 610 3001

Turret Group plc, 177 Hagden Lane, Watford, Herts, WD1 8LN. 01923 228577

VCM Communications, West Orchard, Holmbush Lane, Woodmancote, West Sussex, BN5 9TJ. 01273 857800

Wedding Shows UK Ltd, The Pixmore Centre, Pixmore Avenue, Letchworth, Herts, SG6 1JG. 01462 485881

Westpoint Centre, Clyst St Mary, Exeter, Devon, EX5 1DJ. 01392 444777

Westrade Group, 28 Church Street, Rickmansworth, Herts, WD3 1DD. 01923 778311

Please note that this appendix is based on selected extracts from *Conferences and Exhibitions Diary* – see Appendix E: Recommended Reading, page 137. Information is reproduced with the permission of the publisher, Themetree Limited.

Details are believed to be correct as at 1 November 1996 but are liable to change at any time. You may wish to subscribe to *Conferences and Exhibitions Diary* for fuller information and regular updates.

Inclusion within this appendix does not necessarily constitute a recommendation for the firms listed and you should take sensible precautions and professional advice before entering into business arrangements with them.

# Appendix C: Exhibition services

For quick reference, exhibition services are grouped under these headings:

Audiovisual/Video
Consultants
Contractors
Demonstrators/Models/Dressers/Interpreters
Designers
Display specialists
Electrical contractors
Fireworks
Flags and banners
Floorcoverings/Carpets
Floral displays
Freighting/Transport

Furniture and furnishings
Graphic specialists
Marquees/Tents
Mobile stands/Trailers
Model makers
Modular stands
Photographic
Printers
Promotional goods
Refrigeration
Registration/Evaluation

**Audiovisual/Video**
A1 Video & Audio Visual Hire Services –
    0171 224 3342
Drase Lighting & Special Effects – 01582
    475614
Go Virtual Ltd – 01442 233030
IWM Business Ltd – 0181 964 8020
Istead Business Presentations Ltd – 01203
    635530
Marcon Presentations – 0181 740 7777
Piccadilly Audio Visual Systems – 0171 538
    1622
Pico Group (Europe) – 0181 755 1191
Rose Bay Film Productions Ltd – 0171 412
    0400

**Consultants**
Absolute Events – 01734 733703
Academy Expo – 0181 667 0307
Aktiv Int'l Exhibitions – 0161 203 5554
Arena Display – 01423 868949
Axis Consultants Ltd – 01480 493000
Ayrshire Tourist Board – 01292 262555
Barsby Prince & Partners Ltd – 0116 284 8448
CBM Visual Communications Ltd – 01793
    541555
Capella Communications Ltd – 01274 306343
Canterbury City Council – 01227 763763
Cardiff Marketing Ltd – 01222 667773
Claire Barker Associates Ltd – 01423 873313
Creation Exhibitions – 0171 353 6892
Crozier-Poole & Redwood Exhibitions –
    01734 394040

Davies Virgo & Associates Ltd – 01784 460737

Design & Display Services – 0181 428 6044

Edinburgh Convention Bureau – 0131 226 6888

Exhibition Surveys Ltd – 01664 67666

Fables Child Care Bureau – 01275 393898

Farebrother & Co (Display) Ltd – 0161 872 1268

Fusion 3D – 0171 603 2368

Ilam Services Ltd – 01491 874222

Istead Business Presentations Ltd – 01203 635530

Jack Restan Displays Ltd – 00353 1 450 6006

Marcon Presentations – 0181 740 7777

Marketing Maidstone – 01622 602262

Northamptonshire Chamber of Commerce – 01604 671200

Pinewood Associates – 0161 707 7076

Plymouth Marketing Bureau Ltd – 01752 261125

Promotional Objectives – 01275 853810

Protean Design Ltd – 01844 238679

Rodway Exhibits Ltd – 0117 947 7222

Roundel Exhibitions Ltd – 0818 221 1211

Sasex Int'l Ltd – 01223 892319

The Original Propshop Ltd – 0181 208 1888

### Contractors

Action House Exhibitions Ltd – 01279 757756

Aktiv Int'l Exhibitions – 0161 203 5554

Ardan Exhibition & Display Services Ltd – 0181 207 4957

Arena Display – 01423 868949

Arts & Sales Exhibition Contracts Ltd – 01993 882256

Aspect Exhibition Services – 01604 700601

Axis Consultants Ltd – 01480 493000

Ayre Exhibitions & Shopfitting Ltd – 0161 308 3924

Barsby Prince & Partners Ltd – 0116 284 8448

Beck Exhibition Services – 0121 780 3314

Black & Edgington Structures – 0181 534 8085

British Turntable Co Ltd – 01204 525626

Camden Furniture Hire – 0181 961 6161

Charles Fisher Staging Ltd – 01765 601604

Cobb Group Ltd – 01582 453308

Dalesgate Exhibitions – 01423 502031

Diamond Exhibitions Ltd – 0121 356 6884

Dimension 8 Ltd – 01633 270808

Display Int'l (UK) Ltd – 0171 379 6140

Douglas Temple Design Int'l – 01202 304641

Expo Systems Ltd – 01923 247000

Expoteam Display Ltd – 01442 212989

Hayden Int'l Ltd – 0116 276 6667

JP Displays & Exhibitions – 01202 715722

Jack Restan Displays Ltd – 00353 1 450 6006

Linnel Ltd – 01924 401103

Modex Exhibitions Ltd – 0181 903 2961

Movley Services – 01423 889673

Plus Two Displays Ltd – 01933 678888

Real Image Displays Ltd – 01258 450225

Rodway Exhibits Ltd – 0117 947 7222

Roundel Exhibitions Ltd – 0181 221 1211

Saturn Exhibition & Film Services – 0181 754 9265

Selfexpo Ltd – 01895 835574

Shelec Services Ltd – 0161 707 9090

Slough Exhibition Company Ltd – 01753 577557

Spot on Exhibition Services Ltd – 01675 443332

Stage Plan London – 0181 944 0899

The Original Propshop Ltd – 0181 208 1888

Trojan Display Ltd – 01203 644323

### Demonstrators/Models/Dressers/Interpreters

Claire Barker Associates Ltd – 01423 873313

First Impressions – 0121 705 2774

Jill Dent Int'l Organisation – 01423 561013

Marney Hobdey Promotions – 0171 381 8899

Touchdown Promotions – 0181 614 8006

### Designers

Abbey Lighting – 01789 400705

Absolute Events – 01734 733703

Action House Exhibitions Ltd – 01279 757756

Advanced Polystyrene Ltd – 0161 724 8080

Aktiv Int'l Exhibitions – 0161 203 5554

Architectural Rigging Ltd – 0181 569 0167

Ardan Exhibition Display Services Ltd – 0181 207 4957

Arts & Sales Exhibition Contracts Ltd – 01993 882256

Barsby Prince Partners Ltd – 0116 284 8448

Capella Communications Ltd – 01274 306343

Charles Fisher Staging Ltd – 01765 601604

Cobb Group Ltd – 01582 453308

Crozier-Poole Redwood Exhibitions – 01734 394040

Dalesgate Exhibitions – 01423 502031

Davies Virgo Associates Ltd – 01784 460737

Diamond Exhibitions Ltd – 0121 356 6884

Display Int'l (UK) Ltd – 0171 379 6140

Displayways – 0181 871 2829

Douglas Temple Design Int'l – 01202 304641

ESM Ltd – 01474 536360

Flying Pig Design – 01483 453333

Fusion 3D – 0171 603 2368

Go Virtual Ltd – 01442 233030

Hayden Int'l Ltd – 0116 276 6667

Linnel Ltd – 01924 401103

Marler Haley Exposystems Ltd – 01480 218588

Pico Group (Europe) – 0181 755 1191

Plus Two Displays Ltd – 01933 678888

Protean Design Ltd – 01844 238679

Roundel Exhibitions Ltd – 0181 221 1211

Sasex Int'l Ltd – 01223 892319

Selfexpo Ltd – 01895 835574

Silver Lining Studio Ltd – 01908 630235

Slough Exhibition Company Ltd – 01753 577557

Stand Style – 0171 586 5807

The Original Propshop Ltd – 0181 208 1888

Trojan Display Ltd – 01203 644323

**Display specialists**

Action House Exhibitions Ltd – 01279 757756

Almik Signs Ltd – 0181 743 1090

Arena Display – 01423 868949

Ayre Exhibitions & Shopfitting Ltd – 0161 308 3924

B. Brown Display Materials – 0171 696 0007

Blyco Displays (UK) Ltd – 01707 376555

British Turntable Co Ltd – 01204 525626

Charles Twite & Co Ltd – 0116 278 5391

Dands Sollars – 01452 302755

Displayways – 0181 871 2829

Drase Lighting & Special Effects – 01582 475614

Forge House Models Ltd – 01325 463466

Glazer Plastics Plc – 0181 452 6575

Hayden Int'l Ltd – 0116 276 6667

House of Flags Ltd – 0121 789 7117

Lifestyles – 01993 778077

Marler Haley Exposystems Ltd – 01480 477373

Michael Corgan Ltd – 0181 567 1193

Modex Exhibitions Ltd – 0181 903 2961

Octolight – 0181 530 2610

Pico Group (Europe) – 0181 755 1191

Pinewood Associates – 0161 707 7076

Poppies Exhibitions & Contracts – 01689 845833

Procolor – 0121 550 6430

Promotional Objectives – 01275 853810

Richie Colour Processing Ltd – 0171 837 1259

Roundel Exhibitions – 0181 221 1211

Screen Focus Display Systems – 01792 297 579

Service Graphics Ltd (Teddington) – 0181 943 4488

Silver Lining Studio Ltd – 01980 630235

Slough Exhibition Company Ltd – 01753 577557

Standeasy Modular Display Systems Ltd – 01732 863666

Studio Host Hire – 0171 435 2988

Technographica Int'l – 0181 977 7577

**Electrical contractors**

218 Electrical Services Ltd – 0113 281 3218

Abbey Lighting – 01789 400705

Capella Communications – 01274 306343

Drase Lighting & Special Effects – 01582 475614

ESM Ltd – 01474 536360

Illumination Electrical Contractors Ltd – 0181 207 4957

Melville Exhibition Services Ltd – 0121 780 3022

Shelec Services Ltd – 0161 707 9090

Spot on Exhibition Services Ltd – 01675 443332

**Fireworks**

Jago Fireworks Ltd – 01904 491604

Shell Shock Firework Co – 01664 474484

**Flags and banners**

House of Flags Ltd – 0121 789 7117

The House of Flags Ltd – 01480 861678

**Floorcoverings/Carpets**

Budget Hire Services Ltd – 01438 362934

Expocarpets – 01628 530724

Graham Parrish Exhibitions Ltd – 01530 273220

Stanco Furnishings – 0181 743 6025

**Floral displays**

A1 Creative Cascades – 0171 224 3342

A1 Video Services – 01708 756565

Denbe Display Ltd – 01222 460650

Expo Flora Ltd – 01789 470847

Graham Parrish Exhibitions Ltd – 01530 273220

Hirequirements Ltd – 0161 848 7208

Melville Exhibition Services Ltd – 0121 780 3022

Peebles Exhibition Florists Ltd – 01676 542234

Poppies Exhibitions & Contracts – 01689 845833

Stand Style – 0171 586 5807

**Freighting/Transport**

GBH Exhibition Forwarding Ltd – 0114 269 0641

Rawlings Refrigeration Hire – 0117 942 4417

**Furniture and furnishings**

Architectural Rigging Ltd – 0181 569 0167

Black & Edgington Structures – 0181 534 8085

Budget Hire Services Ltd – 01483 362934

Camden Furniture Hire – 0181 961 6161

Denbe Display Ltd – 01222 460650

Graham Parrish Exhibitions Ltd – 01530 273220

Hirequirements Ltd – 0161 848 7208

John Decamps Ltd – 01283 703161

M & B Marquees East Midlands – 01476 76788

Mahood Marquees – 01744 884158

Melville Exhibition Services Ltd – 0121 780 3022

Portable Floormakers Ltd – 01509 673753

Spot on Exhibition Services Ltd – 01675 443332

Stand Style – 0171 586 5807

**Graphic specialists**

Academy Expo – 0181 667 0307

Almik Signs Ltd – 0181 743 1090

Beck Exhibition Services – 0121 780 3314

CBM Visual Communications Ltd – 01793 541555

Davies Virgo & Associates Ltd – 01784 460737

Design & Display Services – 0181 428 6044

Diamond Exhibitions Ltd – 0121 356 6884

Displayways – 0181 871 2829

Douglas Temple Design Int'l – 01202 304641

Flying Pig Design – 01483 453333

House of Flags Ltd – 0121 789 7117

Perton Signs – 0181 741 4422

Real Image Displays Ltd – 01258 450225

Richie Colour Processing Ltd – 0171 837 1259

Service Graphics Ltd – 01722 321736

Service Graphics Ltd (Teddington) – 0181 943 4488

Service Photography & Display Ltd – 0181 874 4152

Standeasy Modular Display Systems Ltd – 01732 863666

Technographica Int'l – 0181 977 7577

## Marquees/Tents

Atlantic Int'l Tent Hire – 01480 497747
Black & Edgington Structures – 0181 534 8085
M & B Marquees East Midlands – 01476 76788
Mahood Marquees – 01744 884158
Owen Brown Ltd – 01332 850000
Showplace Ltd – 0121 722 3076

## Mobile stands/Trailers

Creation Exhibitions – 0171 353 6892
JP Displays & Exhibitions – 01202 715722
Plus Two Displays Ltd – 01933 678888
Rawlings Refrigeration Hire – 0117 942 4417
Showplace Ltd – 0121 722 3076

## Model makers

Albatross Models, Sets & Affects – 0181 943 4720
Almik Signs Ltd – 0181 743 1090
Dands Sollars – 01452 302755
Forge House Models Ltd – 01325 463466
Silver Lining Studio Ltd – 01980 630235
The Original Propshop – 0181 208 1888

## Modular stands

Academy Expo – 0181 667 0307
Architectural Rigging Ltd – 0181 569 0167
Ardan Exhibition & Display Services Ltd – 0181 207 4957
Aspect Exhibition Services – 01604 700601
Beck Exhibition Services – 0121 780 3314
Clip Display Systems – 0117 937 2636
Cobb Group Ltd – 01582 453308
Dalesgate Exhibitions – 01423 502031
Denbe Display Ltd – 01222 460650
Dimension 8 Ltd – 01633 270808
Display Int'l (UK) Ltd – 0171 379 6140
ESM Ltd – 01474 536360 – 01474 535822
Expo-Link – 01633 489191
Hirequirements Ltd – 0161 848 7208
JP Displays & Exhibitions – 01202 715722
Jack Restan Displays Ltd – 00353 1 450 6006
Lettner GB Ltd – 01604 230445

Linnel Ltd – 01924 401103
Marler Haley Exposystems Ltd – 01480 477373
Modulations – 0181 428 6044
Pinewood Associates – 0161 707 7076
Protean Design Ltd – 01844 238679
RT Display Systems Ltd – 0171 731 4181
Rodway Exhibits Ltd – 0117 947 7222
SD Systems Ltd – 01494 465212
Screen Focus Display Systems – 01792 297579
Selfexpo Ltd – 01895 835574
Service Graphics – 01722 321736
Service Graphics Ltd (Teddington) – 0181 943 4488
Service Photography & Display Ltd – 0181 874 4152
Standeasy Modular Display Systems Ltd – 01732 863666
Taylor Robinson Associates Ltd – 01476 590291

## Photographic

Apollo Photographers Ltd – 0171 603 5051
CBM Visual Communications Ltd – 01793 541555
Perton Signs – 0181 741 4422
Post Studios Photographic – 0121 233 2252
Profot Exhibition & Display Services – 0171 261 9277
Richie Colour Processing Ltd – 0171 837 1259
Service Graphics Ltd – 01722 321736
Service Photography & Display Ltd – 0181 874 4152

## Printers

Copyrite Litho – 01734 814020
Kahn Displays Ltd – 0171 387 9850
Profot Exhibition & Display Services – 0171 261 9277

## Promotional goods

Airborne Packaging Ltd – 0116 253 6136
Bags of Choice – 01772 623703

Glazer Plastics plc – 0181 452 6575
Kahn Displays Ltd – 0171 387 9850
Perton Signs – 0181 741 4422
Quality Badge – 0181 977 7321
Spectra Plastics Ltd – 01926 812195

**Refrigeration**
County Refrigeration Ltd – 0121 643 8048
Lowe Refrigeration – 01232 812248

**Registration/Evaluation**
B & L Systems Ltd – 0181 390 3934
Broad Knowledge Systems Ltd – 0131 557 1565
Exhibition Services Ltd – 01664 67666
Expo-Systems Ltd – 01923 247000
Words Bureau Services & Words Software Systems – 01926 330209

Please note that this appendix is based on selected extracts from *Conferences and Exhibitions Diary* – see Appendix E: Recommended Reading, page 137. Information is reproduced with the permission of the publisher, Themetree Limited.

Details are believed to be correct as at 1 November 1996 but are liable to change at any time. You may wish to subscribe to *Conferences and Exhibitions Diary* for fuller information and regular updates.

Inclusion within this appendix does not necessarily constitute a recommendation for the firms listed and you should take sensible precautions and professional advice before entering into business arrangements with them.

# Appendix D:
# Useful contacts

Agricultural Show Exhibitors Association, 7 Nursery Close, Chadwell Heath, Romford, Essex RM6 4LB. 0181 597 1423.

Association of British Chambers of Commerce, Tufton Street, London SW1P 3QB. 0171 222 1555.

Association of British Market Research Companies, 67 Caledonia Road, London N1 9BT. 0181 977 6905.

Association of Exhibition Organisers, 417 Market Towers, Nine Elms Lane, London SW8 5NQ. 0171 627 3946.

Association of Illustrators, 1 Colville Place, London W1P 1HN. 0171 636 4100.

Association of Market Survey Organizations, Millward Brown International, Olympus Avenue, Tachbrook Park, Warwick, Warwickshire CV34 6RJ. 01926 452233.

Audit Bureau of Circulations Limited, Black Prince Yard, 207-209 High Street, Berkhamsted, Hertfordshire HP4 1AD. 01442 870800.

British Exhibition Contractors Association, Kingsmere House, Graham Road, London SW19 3SR. 0181 543 3888,

British Exhibition Venues Association, Mallards, Five Ashes, Mayfield, Sussex TN20 6NN. 01435 872244.

British Institute of Professional Photography, 2 Amwell End, Ware, Hertfordshire SG1 2HN. 01920 464011.

British Printing Industries Federation, 11 Bedford Row, London WC1R 4DX. 0171 242 6904.

CBD Research Limited, 15 Wickham Road, Beckenham, Kent BR3 2JS. 0181 650 7745.

Central Statistical Office, Great George Street, London SW1P 3AQ. 0171 270 3000.

Chartered Society of Designers, 29 Bedford Square, London WC1 3EG. 0171 631 1510.

Department of Trade and Industry, Ashdown House, 123 Victoria Street, London SE1E 6RB. 0171 215 5000.

Exhibition Audience Audits, 2 Clapham Road, London SW9 0JA. 0171 582 5155.

Exhibition Industries Federation, 115 Hartington Road, London SW8 2HB. 0171 498 3306.

Exhibition Surveys Limited, PO Box 7, Melton Mowbray, Leicestershire, LE13 0BR. 01664 67666.

Her Majesty's Stationery Office, St Crispins, Duke Street, Norwich, Norfolk NR3 1PD. 01603 622211.

Incorporated Society of British Advertisers Limited, 44 Hertford Street, London W1Y 8AE. 0171 499 7502.

Industrial Development Board, 64 Chichester Street, Belfast BT1 4JX. 01232 233233.

London Business School, Sussex Place, Regents Park, London NW1 4SA. 0171 262 5050.

Market Research Society, 12 Northgate Street, London EC1V 4AH. 0171 490 4911.

National Exhibitors Association, 29a Market Square, Biggleswade, Bedford-shire SG18 8AQ. 01767 316255.

Science Reference Library, 25 Southampton Buildings, Chancery Lane, London WC2A 1AN . Telephone : 0171 405 8721.

Society of Typographic Designers, 21-27 Seagrave Road, London SW6 1RP. 0171 381 4258.

# Appendix E: Recommended reading

There are numerous publications available that are relevant to a would-be exhibitor. The following are particularly useful:

## Books

*A Practical Guide to Project Planning* by Celia Burton and Norma Michael. £14.95. Published by Kogan Page, 120 Pentonville Road, London N1 9JN. Telephone: 0171 278 0433. A good introductory read for those business owners and managers who are planning a project, such as exhibiting at an event. It provides a clear and concise overview of the approach required.

*The Effective Use of Market Research* by Robin Birn. £12.95. Published by Kogan Page, 120 Pentonville Road, London N1 9JN. Telephone: 0171 278 0433. An easily absorbed book which combines knowledge and common sense in a straightforward manner.

*Researching Business Markets* edited by Ken Sutherland. £19.95. Published by Kogan Page, 120 Pentonville Road, London N1 9JN. Telephone: 0171 278 0433. This is an excellent source of reference for those who need to collect business data and wish to do so in the correct, effective way.

*Budgeting* by Terry Dickey. £9.99. Published by Kogan Page, 120 Pentonville Road, London N1 9JN. Telephone: 0171 278 0433. This book is a useful and practical guide to financial planning and may help business owners and managers to budget more accurately – an essential skill for prospective exhibitors!

*Creative People* by Winston Fletcher. £14.95 Published by Random House, 20 Vauxhall Bridge Road, London SW1V 2SA. Telephone: 0171 973 9670. A valuable book, looking at creative people and how to handle them. A worthwhile read for anyone who is thinking of using specialists in some capacity.

*How to Perfect Your Selling Skills* by Pat Weymes. £7.99. Published by Kogan Page, 120 Pentonville Road, London N1 9JN. Telephone: 0171 278 0433. An informative guide, setting out the basics of selling. It should be read by sales-people on an exhibition stand.

*Dealing with Demanding Customers* by David M. Martin. £15.99. Published by Pitman Publishing, 128 Long Acre, London WC2E 9AN. Telephone: 0171 379 7383. A useful book, explaining how to handle problem customers – and there will always be one or two of these on every exhibition stand!

## Magazines

*Conferences and Exhibitions Fact Finder.* Free within the industry. Published by Batiste Publications, Pembroke House, Campsbourne Road, London N8 7PE. Telephone: 0181 340 3291. Issued monthly, this magazine incorporates comments, features and up-to-date news on conferences and exhibitions, venues, services and so on. Ask for a copy, although it is more likely to be an interesting, rather than an essential, read.

*Exhibition Management.* £32.90 per annum United Kingdom, £33.80 overseas. Published by FMJ International Publications, Queensway House, 2 Queensway, Redhill, Surrey RH1 1QS. Telephone: 01737 768611. A bi-monthly publication providing news, comments and other details about the exhibition industry. An informative read, and well worth sending for with a view to subscribing to it.

## Miscellaneous publications

*Conferences and Exhibitions Diary.* £75.00 per annum. Published by Theme-tree, 2 Prebendal Court, Oxford Road, Aylesbury, Buckinghamshire HP19 3EY. Telephone: 01296 28585. Published quarterly, this diary allows easy access to facts about forthcoming exhibitions planned in the United Kingdom and Europe, as well as details of organizers, services and so forth. An excellent, value-for-money source of reference.

*Exhibition Bulletin.* £56.00 per annum United Kingdom, £64.00 overseas. Published by The London Bureau, 266–272 Kirkdale, London SE26 4RZ. Telephone: 0181 778 2288. This is a monthly brochure which lists upcoming exhibitions in the United Kingdom and overseas, and also includes an extensive directory of services. It is a quality publication.

*The Exhibition Selector Pack.* Free. Published by Target Response, 1 Riverside, Church Street, Edenbridge, Kent TN8 5BH. Telephone: 01732 866122. Available twice yearly, this pack consists of A4 colour sheets detailing manufacturers and suppliers of equipment and services which can help you to create a winning stand. Each sheet folds into a pre-paid envelope for the relevant advertiser. Well worth requesting.

Please note that the books listed here should be available from your local bookshop and/or library. If not, contact the relevant publisher. Request a free copy of each of the magazines and miscellaneous publications listed, before subscribing to those which are likely to be of ongoing use to you. All prices quoted are correct for 1996 but are subject to change in due course.

# Glossary

Many of the terms used in this book are self-explanatory. Others are less so, and are included here.

*Appropriation.* Sum of money set aside for exhibition activities. More commonly known as a 'budget'.

*Budget.* See 'Appropriation'.

*Business exhibition.* See 'Trade shows'.

*Certificate of Attendance.* Certificate verifying the numbers and types of visitors at an exhibition plus other miscellaneous data.

*Consumer exhibitions.* Exhibitions of widespread appeal; attended by the trade and general public.

*Contractors.* Those specialists responsible for building exhibition stands and other, associated duties such as painting and cleaning.

*Demographics.* Study of the make-up of a population, by age, sex, and so on.

*Designers.* Those experts who design exhibition stands, advise on display items, and supervise their construction, installation and removal from the exhibition.

*Floor plan.* Document showing the scale and layout of the exhibition and its stands. Also known as a hall plan.

*Free-build stand.* Individually designed stand.

*Private exhibitions.* Self-organized exhibitions arranged for trade and/or public visitors.

*Public exhibitions.* Events of interest mainly to the general public.

*Shell scheme.* Rented, standardized unit comprising ceiling, walls and floor.

*Space application form.* Document used by exhibitors to book space at an exhibition. Better known simply as a booking form.

*Technical exhibitions.* See 'Trade shows'.

*Trade shows.* Exhibitions for a particular trade or industry; or specific groups of people working in different industries.

# Index